THE MOST
INCREDIBLE SPORTS STORIES
EVER TOLD

Inspirational and Unforgettable
Tales from the Greatest Athletes Ever

Hank Patton

CONTENTS

ATTENTION:

**DO YOU WANT MY FUTURE BOOKS AT
HEAVY DISCOUNTS AND EVEN FOR FREE?**

**HEAD OVER TO WWW.SECRETREADS.COM
AND JOIN MY SECRET BOOK CLUB!**

INTRODUCTION

The world of sports has held the attention of spectators for thousands of years. People have gone to the coliseums of the world to watch athletes or warriors fight and battle, sometimes for their lives. This form of entertainment has done nothing but grow in popularity throughout human history, with the added benefit of news and television broadcasts to enrich the stories behind the competitors.

When a fan becomes invested in a particular player or team, they come to appreciate the minute details of the big moments. However, over time, those tiny details don't make it into the headlines, or the bullet-pointed lists often found on the internet. When those details are lost or forgotten, some of the luster is stripped away from the incredible story.

This book seeks to keep those important details alive.

Covering multiple sports and many different decades, this book seeks to show readers some of the most incredible, amazing sports stories to ever happen. Whether it be soccer, football, baseball, basketball, ice hockey, golf, boxing, or even auto racing, this book has a story that will keep you interested and turning the pages for more.

We'll see some of the best comebacks of all time, some of the most improbable victories to ever take place, and some of the most dominant performances ever accomplished. By the end, you'll likely have a greater appreciation for these teams and athletes, because their accomplishments are truly incredible.

Even if you are not interested in some of these sports, you will still find these moments entertaining and worth your time, because each one includes a competitive spirit that has lasted all these years.

Whether it is Tiger Woods, Brandi Chastain, LeBron James, and other modern athletes, or those from a more distant past, like Jackie Robinson, the 1969 Mets, or the 1951 Giants, these moments will show that greatness has no age.

Without any further ado, please enjoy each of these true, historically accurate sports stories and the people who were involved with them. Maybe you'll learn something you didn't know about your favorite sport or that iconic athlete that you thought you knew quite well. Enjoy!

CHAPTER 1:

MICHAEL JORDAN WINS HIS SIXTH

In the world of professional basketball, there are a few names that rise to the top of any "greatest player of all time" conversations. Arguably, the name that is most often put at the very top of that list, especially in the past 30 years, is Michael Jordan. For those who were not able to watch him play, it is difficult to comprehend the sheer dominance that Jordan demonstrated over his opponents throughout his career.

With a career so full of big moments, and so many examples of his greatness, it can be difficult to pick the best one. Yet, although he had a long and storied career, no moment better captures Jordan's greatness than the final shot he ever took as a member of the Chicago Bulls.

Let's take a look at this pivotal moment in Michael Jordan's career, and how it helped define his greatness for generations to come.

The scene is the 1998 NBA Finals, where the Chicago Bulls are in a close series with the Utah Jazz. Jordan and his teammates have a chance to win the title on the road in Game 6, but the Jazz have the lead late in the fourth quarter. Fans around the league know that when Michael Jordan is on the floor, anything can happen, but the odds are not in his team's favor.

But why would this championship in particular mean so much to Jordan's legacy? Let's examine what Jordan and the Bulls had accomplished over the last eight years for this single moment to mean so much.

Michael Jordan was drafted in the third overall pick in the 1984 draft by the Chicago Bulls, joining a troubled team that was in desperate need of a turnaround. Jordan was just what they needed, and it didn't take him long to make his impact on the league. In his third season with the team, he led the league in scoring, averaging just over 37 points per game.

When it came to the playoffs, though, Jordan's Bulls struggled to advance past their archrivals in the conference, the Detroit Pistons. Jordan would continue to lead the league in scoring every single season, but it was not until the 1991 playoffs that the Bulls would finally break through and win a championship. Michael Jordan was named the MVP, and the city celebrated. Jordan and the Bulls would go on to win two more championships, making it three in a row.

Then, to the surprise of the entire sports world, Michael Jordan decided to walk away from the game of basketball, reasoning that he had lost the desire to play the game. His decision was also influenced by the murder of his father during that summer, and his exhaustion from having played in the 1992 Olympics. While many people were sad to see him leave the game, the sports world was even more confused by what he decided to pursue next: a career in professional baseball.

Jordan signed a Minor League Contract with the Chicago White Sox and reported to the minor league system in March 1994. He led the Birmingham Barons in strikeouts that season, and he was second on the squad in stolen bases. One year after his entry into the world of baseball, Jordan decided to rejoin the Chicago Bulls in the middle of their 1994–1995 season, helping them to the Eastern Conference Finals, where they lost to the Orlando Magic.

Reportedly, Jordan did not enjoy losing in the playoffs. The Bulls added Dennis Rodman to the roster, and the 1995–96 Bulls won

72 regular season games, a record unbroken until the 2015–16 Warriors.

Jordan collected another scoring title and another MVP. Suddenly, after two years away from Jordan's greatness, it seemed that he had picked up exactly where he had left off. The Bulls won the NBA Championship once more, defeating the Seattle SuperSonics in the NBA Finals.

Many began to wonder, after three championships in a row, were Jordan and the Bulls able to do it again? Could Michael Jordan play at the same level that he had three years ago?

You know the story to this point. Jordan and the Bulls won a second-straight NBA Championship in 1997 when they defeated the Utah Jazz in six games, and they returned to the NBA Finals once again in 1998. The Utah Jazz, with Karl Malone and John Stockton, were waiting for the Bulls once again. Through the first five games, the Bulls were able to muster a 3-2 lead, giving them the opportunity to win their third straight championship for the second time in the decade.

As the fourth quarter began to wind down, though, the Jazz found themselves with the lead. John Stockton hit a three-pointer with 41.9 seconds left in the game, giving the Jazz an 86-83 lead. On the following possession, Jordan immediately drove by Bryon Russell to score a layup, cutting the Jazz lead to one point with 37 seconds on the clock.

The Jazz set up their offense, looking to use up some of the clock, but also wanting to add to their lead. Stockton passed the ball down low to Karl Malone, who was set up in the post position. However, Jordan immediately reacted to the play and double-teamed Malone. Jordan came to Malone's other shoulder, and Malone did not know Jordan was there until the ball was swiped out of his hands.

With 20 seconds left in the game, the ball was in the hands of Michael Jordan, with a chance at basketball immortality. Jordan did not pass the ball. His teammates moved to the perimeter, allowing him to decide how he would proceed. With nine seconds left, Jordan drove toward the middle of the court from the left side, and as he reached the top of the key, just inside the three-point line, Jordan pulled up. His defender, Russell, was unable to react quickly enough, thinking that Jordan was going to keep driving toward the basket as he had on the previous play.

Jordan pulled up and took a jump shot with seven seconds left on the game clock, his defender on the floor and looking up hopelessly for a miss. As the ball swished through the rim, Jordan held his shooting pose. With five seconds left in the game, Jordan and the Bulls were one play away from their sixth championship in eight years.

On the next play, Stockton was unable to make the game-winning three-pointer, and the Chicago Bulls clinched that sixth championship. Michael Jordan, in the last 40 seconds of the game, had scored four points and registered a steal, willing his team to victory.

With the last shot he ever took for the Chicago Bulls; Michael Jordan had cemented his place in basketball history. He proved to everyone who doubted him that he wasn't washed up, that he was still the best. He showed the league that his first departure to play baseball didn't mean he was running away from the competition on the court. He was the Finals MVP once more, six times to go with each of his six championships.

Statistically, Michael Jordan was an impressive player on both sides of the court, although his defensive talents took a backseat to his explosive offensive abilities. Because of his two years away from the league, he didn't necessarily gather the massive numbers that players like LeBron James have in their time. However, his six championships, especially the three after his first departure from the league, put his permanent stamp on the NBA as the very best.

Did You Know?

1. Michael Jordan holds the record for the largest donation to the Make a Wish foundation, with a $10 million donation.

2. Jordan would smoke a cigar as a pregame ritual.

3. Jordan starred in the 1996 film *Space Jam* alongside animated characters Bugs Bunny and Daffy Duck.

4. In 1993, a researcher and doctor named a strain of salmonella after Michael.

5. The Miami Heat retired Jordan's number 23 in 2003, even though he never played for them.

6. In 2016, Jordan received the Presidential Medal of Freedom from President Barack Obama.

CHAPTER 2:

LEICESTER CITY WINS PREMIER LEAGUE

The Premier League is one of the most talked about leagues in modern sports. It's the top league for soccer in the country of England, and it operates using a promotion and relegation system. A team that finishes in the bottom three of the Premier League is relegated to the English Football League Championship, the tier just below. The top two teams of the EFL Championship are promoted to the Premier League, and the third promotion spot is determined by a playoff.

In the history of the Premier League, which was established in 1992, only seven different teams have won the league title, even though 51 different teams have competed in the league over those years.

Relegation is often seen as a moment of disgrace for a team, and it can often cause a team to lose fans, money, and quality players. Still, it happens every season, and this story picks up near the end of one of these seasons, the 2014–2015 year, when Leicester City was on the verge of relegation.

It had been a disappointing season, especially since Leicester City was playing in the Premier League for the first time in ten years. So, when relegation became a possibility, many fans were discouraged by the prospect.

With seven games left in the season, they were in the relegation zone. However, six of those nine games were home games, so the team knew that they had a chance. In a series of performances that became known as the "Great Escape," the Foxes of Leicester City went on a hot streak, winning seven of those nine games, earning one draw, and only suffering one loss to close the season. The team finished 14th out of 20 teams, comfortably out of the relegation zone, which would allow them to continue playing in the Premier League for the next season.

Still, it was not a strong overall performance, so as the team geared up for the 2015–16 season, oddsmakers gave the team a 5,000-to-1 chance to win the league title.

One of the biggest changes the team made in the offseason was at the manager position. The team dismissed Nigel Pearson, known for his fiery temper, and replaced him with Claudio Ranieri, an Italian manager who had a reputation for being much more lighthearted.

The change did not inspire confidence in any analysts or fans, though, as Ranieri had recently been fired as the coach of the Greece national squad after losing to the lowly Faroe Islands team.

To open the season, Leicester scored victories against Sunderland and West Ham United, followed by draws against Tottenham Hotspur and Bournemouth. A victory against Aston Villa and a draw against Stoke City meant the team was unbeaten six games into the campaign.

The first blemish on the squad's record came in their seventh contest when they were soundly defeated on their home turf by Arsenal, 5-2. Remember how we mentioned that only seven teams have ever won the Premier League? Arsenal is one of those seven teams, and they have won it three times, so it would have been no surprise for Leicester City to drop a game against that strong squad.

A signature victory for the squad came during game 16 of the campaign, when they defeated Chelsea 2-1. It was the kind of win that proved Leicester deserved to be near the top of the table. It also helped that Jamie Vardy, the team's striker, broke a league record by scoring in 11 straight matches in the first half of the season.

Now, this was not a team that was blowing away the rest of the league. They did not have the league's highest scorer, nor did they have the cleanest sheets, or even the longest winning streak. What they did have was consistency, and a strong knack to earn points against the best teams in the league.

After that first loss in Game 7 of the campaign, Leicester did not lose again until game 18 against Liverpool, which was the only game of the season in which they did not score. In fact, out of the entire 38-game season, Leicester only lost three matches in total. Their third loss came in the 26th game of the season, and it was their second loss to Arsenal. But before that loss, they scored great victories against Manchester City, Liverpool, and Tottenham.

Draws against Manchester United and Chelsea, plus one more victory against Everton sealed the title for Leicester City, adding them to the list of only seven teams that have won the league.

They overcame the odds placed on them at the beginning of the season. They learned from the mistakes they had made the season before, and more importantly, they maintained the momentum they had gained at the end of the previous season. When Leicester performed their Great Escape to avoid relegation, it spurred them to continue pushing forward.

Finally, a team that was not Manchester United, Manchester City, Chelsea, or Arsenal did not win the Premier League.

With the victory came many accolades from around the soccer world. Jamie Vardy's scoring was recognized by players across the league, as he finished one goal behind Harry Kane for the scoring lead, and he was tied at 24 goals with Sergio Aguero of Manchester City for second place.

The bigger story for the team was Riyad Mahrez, who scored 17 goals for the team and was awarded the Professional Footballers' Association Men's Players' Player of the Year, which is a kind of MVP award voted on by the players' trade union. He became the first African and Algerian player to win the award.

The team received congratulations from across the soccer world, including the Prime Ministers of both the United Kingdom and Italy, as the team was based in the UK with an Italian manager.

Former Leicester striker Gary Lineker had to pay up on a bet he made, appearing in only a pair of boxer shorts to host his BBC show, *Match of the Day*. He admitted that there were no odds he would have taken at the beginning of the year for a bet that Leicester City could win but win they did.

Some wondered if there was some sort of superstitious reason for the team's success, as there had been rumors of the team's owners, who were from Thailand, getting Buddhist monks to bless the players and the team. Coincidentally, King Richard III was also reburied in March of that year, leaving some to wonder if that had any effect on the team.

No matter how the team was able to win their games - and draw against some of their tougher opponents - the fact remains that Leicester City's march to victory in the Premier League remains one of the most improbable and incredible moments in recent soccer history. Speaking of those odds mentioned earlier, it was estimated that gambling businesses in England lost about 25 million pounds to people who had bet on Leicester City to win. One bettor even won 200,000 pounds on their own, all because of a 100-pound bet after the odds had improved to 2000-to-1.

In a league that struggles to find parity due to no restrictions on spending, it is a welcomed sight when one of the teams usually at the middle or bottom of the table rises to the top and find victory. When those moments happen, they capture the imagination of every young player watching the game, knowing they could have a chance at victory, no matter how underrated their team may be.

Did You Know?

1. Leicester City was never lower than sixth in the standings during their winning season.

2. Leicester's point total was less than the previous five winners of the league.

3. Leicester used fewer players than any other team that season, often starting with the same lineup.

4. The budget for Leicester's organization is around a quarter of the budget afforded to Manchester United.

5. Leicester's possession percentage on the season was only 42.4, a low number for a team that performed so well.

6. Their passing percentage was also low, as only one other team in the league completed a lower percentage of their passes.

CHAPTER 3:

THE HELMET CATCH

The world of sports is often ruled by the tiniest of increments. Big moments on the biggest stages often come down to one crucial play, which is often successful or unsuccessful by the smallest of margins. That is the beauty and tragedy of sports. Because of how close victory or defeat can be at any moment in a contest, achieving perfection is nearly impossible. The odds of it happening are just not fantastic. That's why, in the entire history of professional football, it has only been done once. This chapter examines the moment when another team, the 2007–08 New England Patriots, came within inches of becoming the second team in football history to achieve the perfect season.

The story takes place during that 2007–08 season, when the Patriots were returning to the field after a successful 12-4 season the previous year, losing in the AFC Championship to Peyton Manning and the Indianapolis Colts. Still, the team was hungry for more, and they came out swinging.

The team won their first two regular season games by the same score, 38-14, over the New York Jets and San Diego Chargers. Even better, they won 38-7 against the Buffalo Bills in Week 3. They also plowed through the Bengals, Browns, Cowboys, Dolphins, and Redskins, reaching the halfway point of the season with an undefeated record of 8-0. Of those eight games, the only one they didn't win by 20 was against the Browns, where they only won by 17.

The Patriots were dominant, and they were putting the rest of the NFL on notice. In Week 9, they avenged their loss in the AFC Championship from the previous season by defeating the Colts, in Indianapolis, with a close 24-20 score.

As the season wore on, though, the games began to be much closer on the scoreboard. Teams were starting to figure out ways to slow down the Patriots' offense, and suddenly the dominance was feeling not so much of a sure thing. After crushing the lowly Bills again in Week 11 following the Patriots' bye week, Tom Brady and company squeaked by the Philadelphia Eagles, 31-28. It was another three-point victory in Week 13 against the Baltimore Ravens, 27-24, bringing the Patriots' record to 12-0. Just four games from regular season perfection.

They handled the Pittsburgh Steelers at home in Week 14, winning by 21, then they defeated the Jets 20-10 and the Dolphins 28-7. Their record was 15-0, just one game remaining. New England traveled to New York once more to play the 10-5 Giants, who had already secured a playoff spot but were looking to stay sharp for their upcoming Wild Card game.

The game was keenly contested, but the Patriots pulled off the incredible and won the game 38-35, capping a perfect regular season.

When a team perfectly finishes the regular season, they're obviously the favorites to win the championship, and they are likely to feel confident about their chances to do so. After all, the Patriots were the first team in NFL history to go 16-0 since the league adopted a 16-game schedule in 1978. Even more importantly, they had defeated some very good teams on their way to the playoffs.

Still, there were three games to go before perfection on the level of the 1972 Dolphins could be made, and they started with a win in the divisional round against the Jacksonville Jaguars, leaving them one victory from the Super Bowl. Then, in the AFC Championship, the Patriots took care of business against the San Diego Chargers.

One win away from history, the Patriots entered the Super Bowl against a familiar opponent: the New York Giants. It was the team that New England had barely beaten in Week 17, just a few weeks earlier.

Could they find one more victory when it mattered most?

As the Super Bowl game progressed, both teams played well on both sides of the ball, and the score was much lower than their previous matchup. The Giants struck first with a field goal in the first quarter, but the Patriots responded with a touchdown to take the lead going into half-time. There was no scoring in the third quarter, but the Giants struck in the fourth quarter for a touchdown, taking the lead, 10-7. As the clock ticked down under three minutes left in the game, the Patriots were driving deep into the Giants' territory, looking for the go-ahead score.

With 2:45 minutes left, the Patriots had third-and-goal from the Giants' six-yard line when Tom Brady found Randy Moss with the touchdown pass, giving New England the late lead and little chance for New York to mount a comeback.

On the ensuing kickoff, the Giants were stopped at their own 17, giving them terrible field position and needing a touchdown to win. Eli Manning found Toomer for 11 yards, getting out to the 28-yard line. His next pass attempt was over the head of Plaxico Burress. On second down, Manning threw too high once more.

The Giants were likely in four-down territory, meaning they would risk a turnover to get a first down if necessary. But on third down, Manning completed a pass to Toomer over the middle, but Toomer was marked a yard short of the first down.

On the fourth down attempt, Brandon Jacobs was able to gain the one yard needed for a new set of downs, but the clock was ticking, with less than 90 seconds remaining in the game.

On the next first down, Manning was flushed from the pocket, but he gained a few yards before being tackled from behind, nearly losing the ball in the process. On second down, Manning nearly threw an interception, as there was a miscommunication between him and David Tyree.

It was third down once more, five yards to go, and only 75 seconds until a New England Patriots victory. Manning was lined up in the shotgun with two receivers wide, one on each side, one receiver in the slot to his left, while his tight end was lined up on the right edge. His running back was to his right but flared out to run a route after the snap.

When the ball was snapped, the four New England linemen got a quick jump and almost immediately put pressure on Manning, collapsing the pocket.

With two linemen trying to bring him down, one with a handful of Manning's jersey, he somehow slipped away and to the right, buying himself two more seconds. As three more Patriots came barreling toward him, Manning quickly set his feet and fired the football into the air, from the New York 34-yard line to the New England 24-yard line. There were three New England players in the vicinity and one New York Giant.

As David Tyree jumped up for the ball, a New England defender put his hand between the outstretched arms of Tyree. When the ball landed in Tyree's hands, he could not bring it down to his chest to secure it because of the Patriot trying to dislodge it. Instead, Tyree pinned the ball against the top of his helmet as he fell backward onto the New England player, squeezing the ball in place to prevent it from coming loose.

As the two players toppled to the ground, referees signaled that it was a good catch, and the New York Giants had been gifted the stroke of luck they needed to win. They would score a touchdown on another pass to Burress with 35 seconds left, and they held on to defeat the unbeaten Patriots for the Super Bowl victory.

The Giants did the unthinkable, and they needed an incredible play to get it done. Looking back, the play was even more improbable when considering the player involved. David Tyree was not a big-name player in the NFL. In his entire career, which only lasted seven seasons, Tyree had 54 catches for 650 yards and four touchdowns. During that regular season, he only had four catches for 35 yards. This was not a difference-making player on any other day in his career.

But he didn't need to be. He only needed one opportunity to put his stamp on NFL history. One of his 54 career catches, the Helmet Catch, helped the Giants win the Super Bowl and deny the New England Patriots their historical win.

Did You Know?

1. The 2007 Patriots averaged 40 yards and eight points of offense more than the next closest team, making them the best offense in the league.

2. The Patriots' average margin of victory for the first ten games of the season was 25.4 points.

3. The Helmet Catch was the last completion Tyree ever caught in his career.

4. NFL Films named the Helmet Catch the best play of the decade.

5. The play call from the Giants offense was "62 Sail-Y Union."

6. Tyree caught the first Giants touchdown early in the fourth quarter of the game.

CHAPTER 4:

2004 UEFA EUROPEAN FOOTBALL CHAMPIONSHIP

If you are unfamiliar with the tournament known as the UEFA European Championship, or Euro, it's a tournament held every four years that pits European national teams against one another. One team plays host to the other teams in the tournament, each of which must qualify by winning games in their group stages. It is the second-most watched soccer tournament after the World Cup, so it has quite the following.

This chapter focuses on one iteration of this fantastic tournament, which took place in the summer of 2004. Now, because this tournament is comprised of teams that regularly compete for the World Cup every year, it's no surprise that those big teams often factor into the results of this tournament as well. Just think of the teams involved and see if you recognize any of them from World Cup tournaments in the past 30 years: Germany, Spain, Italy, Netherlands, France, Portugal, and more.

However, all of these teams fell short of one squad that proved to be the spoiler of the tournament. Greece played a tournament for the ages, shocking the soccer world and demonstrating that any team can win on one of the world's biggest stages. Let's see how they accomplished the incredible.

The 2004 Euro was hosted by Portugal, who were also favored to do well in the tournament. In Group A, Greece, who were not expected to perform well in the tourney, found themselves having to face the hosts in the first group match. However, Greece rocked the soccer world in their very first fixture when they scored seven minutes into the contest. They followed up their opening goal with a penalty kick goal in the 51st minute, going up 2-0 and surprising everyone in the tournament. Cristiano Ronaldo (Portugal) would score in stoppage time, but it wasn't enough as Greece defeated Portugal 2-1 to open their tournament.

Portugal would recover and win the group with victories over Russia and Spain.

Greece, on the other hand, still had work to do, and they were still not expected to escape the group. Yet, they scored a draw against Spain to help their cause, but they lost to Russia. At the end of the group stage, Greece and Spain were tied with four points each. However, because Greece scored more goals than Spain, they finished second in Group A and advanced to the knockout stage.

At this point in the tournament, with only eight of the 16 teams remaining, the prevailing opinion was that Greece should be happy with their result, but they would likely be wiped out by France, the top team in the world at that time. Instead, with a goal in the 65th minute by Angelos Charisteas, Greece secured one more shocking victory as they advanced to the semi-final.

Waiting for them was the fourth-ranked team in the world, the Czech Republic. This game was even more intense, as both teams reached the end of full-time with no scoring. In extra time for this Euro tournament, any goal is a golden goal, ending the game immediately. Greece put this to good use, as Traianos Dellas scored a header from a corner kick to send Greece to the tournament final.

It was another shock, and the soccer world was buzzing with excitement for the underdog team. Greece only had one game left to come away with the trophy, but the team waiting for them was none other than the tournament hosts, Portugal.

With 62,865 fans watching in the stadium, with millions watching around the world, the two squads faced each other one more time.

This time around, there would not be a shocking goal seven minutes into the match. Instead, Portugal was the aggressive side to begin the match, and Greece had to be a great deal sharper on defense as Miguel registered the first shot on goal for Portugal. Angelos Charisteas had a quality chance of his own two minutes later, then Portugal's Maniche missed from just near the penalty spot.

After the early trade of chances, the two teams settled in defensively and played a closely contested first half, keeping any other scoring opportunities to a minimum. At the half, the score remained tied at zero.

In the second half, Deco appealed for an early penalty call but was denied by the referee. Instead, Greece continued their strong defensive play and took advantage of yet another corner kick set-piece goal, this time headed home by Angelos Charisteas in the 57th minute. It was Greece's first corner kick of the match, and they made it count.

Moments later, Ronaldo had a chance to tie the match once more, but his shot from the edge of the penalty area was saved by Greece's goalkeeper, Antonios Nikopolidis.

With 30 minutes left in the match, Portugal desperately needed to even the score, but as the minutes slowly ticked away, the fans of Greece and all those fans around the world who love an underdog watched as the victory inched closer.

Luis Figo had a quality chance without result minutes later, and Maniche also registered a chance that did not produce a goal for Portugal. Then in the 74th minute, Cristiano Ronaldo found himself in on the Greece goaltender with no defenders between them. Ronaldo's shot went just over the crossbar, keeping Greece's lead intact.

The last 15 minutes of the match were played without any great incident, and Greece held on to win the game and capture the tournament crown, sending an entire country of soccer fans into jubilation.

It marked a significant moment in European football, as many viewed the traditional powerhouse teams as the only ones capable of winning on the big stages. Greece proved those doubters wrong, for one tournament, at least. Pundits around the world considered the game to be the greatest upset in the history of the tournament, and it was an easy argument to make.

Before this championship run, Greece had only qualified for this tournament once before, back in 1980. They had also never won a match at any significant tournament, ever. So, to explode and win four out of six matches against some of the best competition in the world was truly an incredible feat.

As it turns out, though, Greece had been playing with some sort of luck, as they failed to qualify for the World Cup two years later, and they were also unsuccessful in their title defense of the European Championship in 2008. They lost all three of their group-stage matches against Spain, Russia, and Sweden.

Greece's success may not have been the beginning of a great soccer program year after year, like many other European teams have had. Still, their championship win in 2004 was a pleasant surprise for the entire country of Greece. Many soccer fans in that country will tell the incredible story of their one glorious moment against many of the best teams in the world, and it will be a story worth telling until the national team can find that magic once more.

Did You Know?

1. The 2004 Euro was the first to be held in Portugal.

2. Each match averaged over 34,000 fans.

3. Latvia made their first appearance in the tournament.

4. Giorgos Karagounis was suspended for two of Greece's matches because of red cards.

5. Milan Baros of the Czech Republic won the Golden Boot for the tournament with five goals.

6. Theodoros Zagorakis was named the tournament's best player.

CHAPTER 5:

BUSTER DOUGLAS UPSETS MIKE TYSON

It is common knowledge that sporting events can hinge on single moments, and there can be a very thin line between potential victory and defeat. The world of professional boxing is no different. This incredible story focuses on the downfall of one of the best boxers in the history of the sport, Mike Tyson.

A young phenomenon, Mike Tyson's boxing career began as an amateur competitor, where he was already quite successful. He won gold medals at the Junior Olympic Games in both 1981 and 1982. The 1982 match, specifically, was a quick result, with Tyson's opponent throwing in the towel in the first round. Two years later, Tyson won another gold medal, this time at the National Golden Gloves, an amateur competition focused on American boxers.

It was no surprise to those paying attention to the boxing world when Mike Tyson made his professional debut in 1985, scoring a first-round TKO. Over his next 27 fights, he would collect 25 more KO or TKO victories, and 15 of them came in the first round, just like his debut. However, when Tyson's trainer, Cus D'Amato, passed away in November 1985, Tyson began struggling to keep his personal life together.

It did not help that Tyson's early success was very likely too much for a young man to handle. Over the next couple of years, details of his troubled personal life began to appear in news reports and tabloid magazines. Because of these troubles, Tyson dismissed his trainer and manager, and the effect was immediate, with the speedy fighter using fewer defensive tactics and combination punches.

After being the undisputed champion, holding three different belts, and defending his title on multiple occasions, he faced the seventh-ranked Buster Douglas in Tokyo, Japan, on February 11, 1990.

It was reported that both fighters were dealing with adverse situations going into the fight, although their scenarios could not have been more different. Douglas was dealing with the recent death of his mother, and he also contracted the flu the night before the fight. Tyson, on the other hand, was disrespecting his opponent well before the fight even started. He stayed out late the night before, refusing to go to sleep early and drinking with his friends.

Still, the boxing world expected another quick knockout for Tyson. However, Douglas quickly proved that this fight was going to be different. Douglas came out with a lot of movement, throwing punches when he found an opportunity. It also helped that Douglas had a full foot of reach advantage over Tyson, so his jab helped keep Tyson away from him.

During the middle rounds of the fight, Douglas continued to dominate, though he did have to survive a few of Tyson's patented uppercuts along the way. Even more embarrassing, Tyson's corner team didn't bring any ice packs because they weren't expecting to need them. To make up for the lack of ice, they filled rubber gloves with water and held it against Tyson's swollen eye, though its effectiveness was questionable.

Going into the eighth round, Douglas continued to manage the fight, but Tyson hung on. Toward the end of the round, Douglas backed Tyson into the ropes with his jab, looking to finish off the undisputed champion. Instead, Tyson did what he had done so many times before. Another big uppercut from the champion caught the challenger off guard, sending him to the mat.

At this point, there is some dispute about the validity of the referee's count. The knockdown timekeeper at ringside began the count as soon as Douglas' back hit the mat, the referee's count seemed to be two beats behind, giving Douglas more time to get up. Using that time to his advantage, Douglas stumbled to his feet at the referee's count of nine, barely escaping a knockout. The round ended before Tyson could continue his attack, and Douglas had a moment to recover in his corner.

The ninth round began, and Tyson tried to reassert his attack from the end of the previous round, but Douglas was able to defend effectively, and his counterattack caused Tyson's swollen eye to shut completely. As the two fighters traded intense blows, Douglas landed a four-punch combination that had Tyson wobbling on his feet and leaning against the ropes for support. He closed in on the champion and tried to finish the job, but Tyson was able to survive the attack and the round.

With the tables turned, the tenth round began with Tyson once more trying to assert dominance, but his injuries were becoming too much for him to endure. As Tyson tried to push forward, Douglas caught him with jabs and then an uppercut that stopped Tyson's movement, leaving him open to four more punches to the head. For the first time in Mike Tyson's career, he was knocked to the mat.

The boxing world looked on in shock as Tyson fumbled on the mat, trying to grab and put his mouthguard back in as he tried to regain his feet.

The referee continued to count as the audience cheers continued to swell...until the referee reached ten and declared Tyson knocked out!

Despite being a 42-1 underdog, Buster Douglas had pulled off the incredible upset, defeating the boxer who had been in control of the sport for the past few years. It completely shook up the boxing scene, and it forever changed the trajectory of Mike Tyson's career.

When Douglas was interviewed in the ring after the fight, he broke down in tears, saying that his mother was the reason that he had won the fight. Tyson, for his part, declared that the fight was the best thing to happen in his career, because he thought that the loss helped him refocus and take the sport more seriously.

There were talks of a rematch between the two fighters, but those talks fell apart after Douglas lost the titles to Evander Holyfield just four months later. Douglas retired after that loss. He tried to make a comeback six years later, spurred by an incident when he almost died from a diabetic coma. The return spluttered, and he did not participate in another fight after 1999.

As for Tyson, he competed in four more fights before he was convicted of rape, which sent him to prison. When he was released from his sentence, he returned to the boxing scene and won the WBA and WBC world titles very quickly. However, he lost them to Evander Holyfield, never regaining them again.

While Douglas is remembered for his glorious, incredible moment against the best boxer in the world, Mike Tyson is still an active part of American culture. It didn't help that he attracted negative attention for biting Evander Holyfield during their rematch, but he still managed to be relevant in the boxing scene until 2002.

When his competitive career ended, Tyson appeared in various pieces of media, including documentaries, television shows, animated series, feature films, and more. Most famously, Tyson appeared as himself in the film *The Hangover*. He also performed a one-man show both in Las Vegas and on Broadway, where he would talk and joke about his personal and professional life.

Mike Tyson had a prolific boxing career, winning 50 fights, 44 by knockout. He only lost six times over his career. It is incredible that his very first loss came to a man who was not supposed to win. It came to a man who was not expected to survive the first round. And yet, the incredible moment in Tokyo forever changed the trajectory of Tyson's career. Many wonder what could have been if Tyson had not fired his manager and trainer, and instead had remained focused on his career.

The boxing world will never know what could have been, but many will remember Tyson's accolades in the ring fondly all the same.

Did You Know?

1. Douglas was a 42:1 underdog for this fight.

2. Tyson's previous outing was a 93-second knockout of Carl Williams.

3. Before the fight, Tyson was the rare heavyweight fighter considered to be the best pound-for-pound fighter.

4. Douglas had lost his previous title fight but won seven straight after the loss to earn another shot.

5. It was mentioned on the broadcast that Douglas had a dog named Shakespeare.

6. American rock band The Killers wrote a song called "Tyson vs. Douglas," reminiscing about seeing the fight as a child.

CHAPTER 6:

THE 1969 "MIRACLE" METS

In the old days of professional baseball, a losing team was a difficult thing to turn around. If your favorite team had a terrible season, it was a reasonable assumption that the team would struggle for the next few years, if not longer.

So, when a team is able to escape that cycle of losing on a faster-than-usual schedule, it catches the attention of the baseball world. When it happens to a team that has not been playing well for a very long time, then it becomes a legendary story told for years to come.

This is one of those legendary stories.

The New York Mets were preparing to begin their eighth season in existence as part of Major League Baseball. It was also the first year that divisional play was utilized in the league, and the Mets were assigned to the National League East along with The Chicago Cubs, Montreal Expos, Philadelphia Phillies, Pittsburgh Pirates, and St. Louis Cardinals.

Despite the format change, few expected the Mets to have any sort of success during the 1969 season, and for good reason. In their previous eight seasons of existence, the Mets had never finished higher than ninth place out of the ten teams in the National League. The team had never had a winning season, meaning that they always lost more games than they won. During the 1968 season, the Mets only finished ahead of the Houston Astros, winning 73 games to Houston's 72.

The Mets even held the MLB record for the most losses in the 20th century, as they lost 120 games in the 1962 season.

Still, a new season is always a new chance for every team, and the Mets were excited to give it another shot. In fact, their opening day game was a historic moment for the league. It was the first time that two teams from different countries played each other, as the Montreal Expos came to town. The two teams slugged it out, an entertaining game, sure, but the Mets lost 11-10.

It marked the beginning of a not-so-great start for the team, as they would be at three wins and seven losses after ten games, and it was a pace of winning that surprised no one in the league.

After 23 games, it was more of the same, as the team had won nine and lost 14. Now, there were 162 games in the regular season, so there was still more than 80% of the season to go. After those first 23 games, the Mets began to figure things out. Over their next 13 games, they won nine. They even had two shutouts in a row, against the Cubs and Expos. The shutout against the Cubs was particularly notable, as that Chicago team was playing quite well.

Throughout May, the team was 21-23, though they did win seven out of 12 home games. Things were beginning to move in their favor, but there was still work to be done.

From May 28 to June 10 of that season, something quite amazing took place. The Mets won a franchise-record 11 games in a row, sweeping the Giants, Dodgers, and Pirates before finally dropping a game to the Giants on June 11. It was becoming quite clear that the team was on an upward trajectory, thanks to pitcher Tom Seaver, who had already won nine games by this point in the season. By the end of the campaign, he would lead the league in wins with 25. Out of those 25 wins, nine of them were complete games, an impressive feat in any era of baseball.

Running off the momentum from the beginning of the month, the summer looked even better for the Mets. They went 11-9 for the rest of June, and for July, their record was 15-12. This included three losses to the Astros to end the month. Interestingly, by the end of the season, the Houston Astros finished their season with an 81-81 record, and they were the only team in the league to finish with a winning head-to-head record against the Mets.

Every other team in that season would finish with a losing record to the Miracle Mets.

Still, there was work to be done, because the Chicago Cubs were in a great position to win the pennant. Halfway through August, they still had a nine-game lead over the Mets and the Cardinals. But, the months of August and September would give the Mets a chance to show that they still had another level of play to reach. While they went 9-9 on the road in August, they were nearly unbeatable at home. They won 12 games and only lost one.

Not satisfied, and knowing they had to keep ahead of their close rivals in the standings, they were a scorching 23 and seven in September. By the end of the regular season, the Mets had finished with 100 wins, and 62 losses, giving them the second-best record in the league. With their strong performance, they became the first expansion team in the history of the league to reach the postseason. The Baltimore Orioles, over in the American League East, finished with 109 wins and were the favorites to win the World Series.

Even more impressive is how much the Mets inspired fans to get behind their efforts. During the regular season, the Mets finished first in the league for fan attendance, averaging over 26,000 spectators per home game.

With the introduction of divisions to the league, this was the first time in MLB history that there would be a playoff to determine the two teams headed to the World Series. In the past, the team with the best records from the AL and NL would automatically go to the Series. So, even though the Miracle Mets had performed well above past expectations, there was still more they had to accomplish.

In the first MLB playoff series ever played in the deep south of the United States, the Mets faced the Atlanta Braves in a best-of-five series for a chance to reach the World Series. In the first game of the series, the Mets trailed 5-4 in the seventh inning after the Braves found some success against Seaver.

However, in the eighth inning, the Mets exploded for five runs, took a big lead, and held on to win the opening game.

In Game 2, the Mets won another game on the road, 11-6, sending the series back to New York with the Mets having a chance to win the series at home.

In front of their home fans, though, the Mets fell behind by two runs in the first inning, and they had to pull their pitcher after two innings. Then, they put a young Nolan Ryan on the mound, who pitched the rest of the game.

The Mets got one of those runs back in the third, then they took the lead in the fourth with two more runs. In the top of the fifth, the Braves retook the lead with two more runs of their own, but the Mets responded immediately with three runs in the bottom of the inning. They took the lead and shut out the Braves for the rest of the game.

The Mets finished the sweep of the Braves, clearing their path to the World Series. Waiting for them on the other side of the bracket was the first-place Baltimore Orioles, who also swept their opponents, the Minnesota Twins.

To open the series, Baltimore won Game 1, 4-1. However, the Mets responded in Game 2, winning 2-1 and gaining home-field advantage, as the next three games would be in New York. Returning home, the Mets won 5-0, and the shutout was shared between Gentry and Ryan.

Game 4, though, was the big moment in the series. The Mets were leading 2-1 in the series, but a win would put them in a commanding lead, while a loss would tie the series with three games remaining.

The contest was close throughout. The Mets jumped ahead in the second inning, 1-0, and the game went without another score for the next six innings. Then, in the top of the ninth, Baltimore scored on a sacrifice fly to tie the game and send it to extras. In the bottom of the tenth, the Mets scored the winning run when an errant throw hit a baserunner and allowed the runners to advance.

With a commanding 3-1 lead, the baseball world was ready to witness what most consider to be the biggest upset in World Series history.

Again, Baltimore had other ideas, and they struck first. With three runs in the third inning, the Orioles took a strong lead. However, the Mets had shown all season that they had the resilience to respond. In the third, fourth, and fifth innings, the Mets continued to struggle at the plate. Then, in the sixth, New

York got two of those runs back, going into the seventh only behind by one.

Then, in the seventh, the Mets tied the game. Everyone in the stadium was excited for what they considered to be the inevitable: the Mets were going to complete the comeback.

One inning later, they added two more runs, and pitcher Jerry Koosman pitched the complete game to finish the series and win the Mets their first-ever championship.

For the first time in MLB history, an expansion team had won the title, and it was the team that had seemed least likely to do so, based on the last eight years of struggle and pain. It was an incredible moment for the team and the league, and their popularity helped the sport grow even more around the country.

The Miracle Mets demonstrated that every pitch, every inning is important. Even though they fell behind in big games down the stretch, they found ways to battle back. Sometimes, losing for a long time can break a player or a team. Great players and great teams, though, learn to continue pushing through the pain and giving their best at every turn. The 1969 Mets personified these qualities, and they earned a World Series Championship for their incredible efforts.

Did You Know?

1. Former team manager Casey Stengel is credited with giving this Mets team the "Miracle" title.

2. The Mets held their spring training in St. Petersburg, Florida that year.

3. The teams added to the National League that season were the Montreal Expos and the San Diego Padres.

4. Cleon Jones was the team leader in batting average, with a .340.

5. Tom Seaver's 25-win season featured a 2.21 ERA.

6. Center fielder Tommie Agee led the way with 76 RBIs and 26 home runs.

CHAPTER 7:

RONDA ROUSEY

The world of professional fighting has expanded in the past couple of decades thanks to the rise of mixed martial arts, which brings together fighting styles from all around the world to find the best fighters.

Organizations like the Ultimate Fighting Championship, or UFC, have been organizing Pay Per View events on an almost monthly basis for the last few years, bringing more attention to the sport as they continue to gain a following.

Like a boxing card, there are several fights at an event, often culminating in a fight between the top two fighters of a weight division as they battle for the championship belt.

As the sport continued to grow, organizers and promoters realized that there was a market to begin introducing women's divisions for many weight classes, adding them to the lineups along with the men's fights.

The emergence of women's fighting gaining popularity in popular culture coincided with the rise of a very talented judoka by the name of Ronda Rousey. Let's examine the fighting career of Ronda Rousey and how she helped elevate the sport of women's MMA.

When she was just 11 years old, Ronda began learning judo with her mother, and the two of them trained together for two years before she unintentionally broke her mother's wrist. From that moment on, Ronda had to train without her mom.

When she was 17, she became the youngest qualifier for the 2004 Summer Olympics, but she lost her first match to Claudia Heill, who would go on to win the silver medal. Rousey had more success at the World Judo Junior Championships later that year, where she won gold.

At 19 years old, Rousey became the first American judoka in a decade to win at the highest-level tournament when she won the Birmingham World Cup with a 5-0 record. In the same year, she won a bronze medal when she competed at the Junior World Championships. With that result, she became the most decorated U.S. athlete for Junior World medals.

During the next spring, Rousey won the 2007 Pan American Games before coming in second place at the 2007 World Judo Championships. All of this was building up to the 2008 Olympics, where she became the first American to win a medal in women's judo with a bronze.

After her judo career was over, Rousey realized that she didn't want to work regular jobs to survive, so she contacted her old trainers and began working toward a career in MMA.

Two years after her bronze medal, Rousey had her first amateur MMA match, which she won in 23 seconds with an armbar submission. She then entered the Tuff-N-Uff tournament, which was a tournament for amateur competitors looking to make the jump to the professional ranks. Rousey defeated veteran fighter Autumn Richardson in 57 seconds with another armbar, and then she only needed 24 seconds to win in the semi-finals of the tournament.

Instead of finishing that competition, Rousey decided to go pro immediately. Four months later, she made her professional debut against Ediane Gomes, whom she submitted with an armbar in 25 seconds. With these quick, dominant victories, Rousey was gaining attention from fighters and organizations all around the MMA world. Three months after her first victory, she won again, submitting Charmaine Tweet, a kickboxing champion, in 49 seconds with yet another armbar.

Then, it was on to Strikeforce, another fighting organization, and Rousey took no time making an impact. She submitted Sarah D'Alelio quickly in the first round, then did the same to Julia Budd four months later. Then, Rousey dropped down a weight class, from 145 to 135, so she could challenge Miesha Tate for the Bantamweight Championship. On March 3, 2012, Rousey won by armbar in the first round, dislocating Tate's elbow in the process.

With her championship win, the Ultimate Fighting Championship was beginning to take notice. UFC President Dana White did not have any female fighters, but Rousey had gained his attention.

In the meantime, Rousey defended her title against Sarah Kaufman five months later, winning by armbar in 54 seconds. Three months after her title defense, she was offered a contract with the UFC, and she defended her title with the UFC in February 2013. In that fight, Rousey defeated Liz Carmouche 4 minutes and 49 seconds into the first round by armbar. However, it was the first time Rousey had been injured in a fight, as Carmouche had dislocated Rousey's jaw during that first round.

Still, Rousey defended her title again in December 2013, defeating Miesha Tate once more, this time in the third round, but still by an armbar submission.

Rousey would go on to defend her belt four more times, totaling 1,066 seconds in the ring and over a million dollars in prize money for her efforts.

Her reign came to an end when Holly Holm knocked out Rousey in the second round, and her professional fighting career was brought to its knees with the loss. Rousey would later admit she contemplated suicide after the loss, but she recovered and attempted one more comeback, a title shot against the new champion, Amanda Nunes.

That fight resulted in a TKO to Rousey, as Nunes was a much better striker than any other woman in the sport at the time. Nunes, in her post-fight speech, thanked Rousey for her contributions to the sport, in giving women the platform to perform and entertain when no such avenue had existed before.

With the loss, Rousey retired from the sport. She was selected to enter the UFC Hall of Fame 18 months later. With her fighting career over, Rousey turned more toward the entertainment side of American culture, appearing in several films and television shows. She also signed a contract with World Wrestling Entertainment, a professional wrestling organization that creates stories between their wrestlers for entertainment value.

During her time with the WWE, Rousey played a substantial role on the women's roster, winning championships of all kinds and bringing more attention to the women's side of the show. For reference, her debut match took place at WrestleMania 34, which is the largest annual event for the sport, where she defeated Stephanie McMahon by way of her patented armbar technique, though probably not actually used to cause any injury or pain.

Most recently, Rousey was defeated by a wrestler named Shayna Baszler at SummerSlam, another big event, by way of submission. Since then, Rousey has not appeared for WWE, leading some to believe that her career with the organization may be at an end.

To this day, Rousey's impact on women's fighting has been immense and unquestionable. She holds the UFC record for longest title fight finish streak with six, meaning that her fights never went to scorecards. She also holds the record for the fastest women's title fight, when she defeated Cat Zingano in 14 seconds.

Rousey was also recognized as the Best Female Athlete by the ESPY awards in both 2014 and 2015, ahead of other prominent female athletes playing soccer, basketball, tennis, and hockey. This was the true indicator that Rousey had captured the hearts of American sports fans far and wide because few other female sporting events had attracted the kind of attention and money from viewers and fans.

Looking back, some criticize Rousey and question her fighting skills, as she had been quite a one-dimensional fighter in a class of fighters that were not very strong. Her wrestling skills were elite, but when she tried to rely on striking, she was easily outclassed. Still, her positive impact on the sport cannot be denied.

If it were not for Ronda Rousey and her incredible string of dominant victories, the world of women's MMA would likely not be as strong as it is today. Not only did she dominate in the octagon, but she also used her influence to bring more eyes to the sport. She was entertaining at every level, and for a few years, everyone wanted her to win and dominate.

Analysts compare her run to the early years of Mike Tyson's career when fans flocked to watch him decimate his opponents quickly. There is something undeniably entertaining in watching such greatness. Rousey brought that greatness to the world of MMA, much like Tyson did for boxing. Her incredible career will be tough to match for a long time to come.

Did You Know?

1. Ronda was born with her umbilical cord wrapped around her neck, resulting in hypoxia. She struggled to speak for much of her childhood.

2. Ronda often walked to the MMA cage with the song "Bad Reputation" by Joan Jett playing in the arena.

3. Ronda's nickname, "Rowdy," came from Rowdy Roddy Piper, the professional wrestler.

4. Ronda has a brown belt in Brazilian Jiu-Jitsu.

5. TIME Magazine included Ronda on their 2015 list of the "100 Most Influential People."

6. Ronda was the first woman to be featured on the cover of *Men's Fitness* magazine.

CHAPTER 8:

THE MIRACLE ON ICE

The world of sports is often used to escape the pains and worries of everyday life. Fans can focus their attention on their favorite teams and players, and they can enjoy the successes that those athletes earn. Sometimes, though, the real world finds its way into the storyline taking place for those teams and athletes.

This is one such story of a moment when a hockey game between two international hockey teams represented so much more than the numbers on the scoreboard.

The game in question took place during the medal round of the 1980 Winter Olympics in Lake Placid, New York. The two teams involved in the game were the hosts, the United States, and the reigning, four-time defending Olympic champions, the Soviet Union.

The expectation going into the tournament was that the United States would not perform well, as they were not allowed to use NHL players on their roster. They were also very young, as they had the youngest average age of any team in the tournament. The Soviet team, on the other hand, was full of professional players, most of whom had lots of international hockey experience.

Because of their experience, the Soviets were the heavy favorite to win the tournament, just as they had for the four previous Olympic games. On their roster were some of the biggest names in the sport, such as Vladislav Tretiak, who most considered to be the best goaltender in the world. They also had Viacheslav Fetisov, who would later enjoy a successful NHL career. Forward Sergei Makarov was also known for his speed and dynamic play. In fact, all of these Soviet players would later end up in the Hockey Hall of Fame.

The Soviets were so serious about their performance in ice hockey that many of their players were employed by military groups or large companies in Russia, not for their business acumen or any other skill they possessed, but only to play hockey for that organization's team.

When it came to whether this arrangement was fair, there was no arguing with the Olympic Committee. Canada had boycotted the two previous Olympic games in an attempt to prevent Russia's professionals from competing but to no avail.

Instead, the United States had to rely on a roster of entirely new players to the Olympic scene, except for one player, Buzz Schneider, who had competed for the U.S. during the 1976 Games. For the rest of the team, coach Herb Brooks selected nine players that he had personally coached at the University of Minnesota. Reportedly, Brooks gave every player he interviewed a 300-question test to determine how the players would perform in a stressful situation.

Most importantly, eyes were on this tournament because of the events taking place in geopolitics. The Cold War was in full swing, with the Soviets invading Afghanistan just three months earlier. Relations were tense between the two countries as they both continued building bigger and more powerful weaponry.

Because of those tensions, any meetings between the two nations would be closely scrutinized, and that included Olympic hockey. It didn't help the Americans that Soviet teams had been on an exhibition tour across North America, where they defeated NHL teams often, and even took down a team of All-Stars to claim the Challenge Cup.

With all this buildup to the tournament, many were resigned to the conclusion that the Soviets would capture gold once more. Still, there were hockey games to play.

The American team came out strong and surprised the analysts by getting a draw against Sweden before handily defeating Czechoslovakia. Then the U.S. team followed up their strong start with wins over Norway, Romania, and West Germany. Out of that group, the U.S. and Sweden advanced to the medal round.

The Soviets' path to the medal round was easier, as they dominated their opponents. Opening against Japan, the Soviet team scored 16 unanswered goals. Then, facing the Netherlands, the Soviets scored 17, but they did allow four goals against. Poland fared better than some, only losing 8-1. The Soviets then played Finland and Canada, beating both teams by two goals each, 4-2 against Finland and 6-4 over Canada.

Joining the U.S. and Sweden were the Soviet Union and Finland. Unlike modern medal rounds that feature single-elimination brackets, this medal round was a round-robin style. The United States would have to play the two teams from the other group, and their result from tying Sweden would be added to their point total.

If they wanted gold, they needed two wins. First, they had to play the Soviets.

Early in the game, the United States found themselves behind. A slapshot from Alexei Kasatonov was deflected in front of the net by Vladimir Krutov, and U.S. goaltender Jim Craig could not stop the shot. At the halfway point of the period, the Soviets were ahead 1-0. Five minutes later, the only veteran of international play on the U.S. roster, Buzz Schneider, scored on a 50-foot shot from along the boards, tying the game.

Sergei Makarov responded for the Soviets with less than three minutes left in the period, restoring their one-goal lead. Jim Craig responded and played better, helping the U.S. squad weather the Soviet storm until they caught a lucky break near the end of the period.

Dave Christian took a long slapshot on Soviet goalie Tretiak, and while it was an easy save, Tretiak misplayed the rebound, which was collected by Mark Johnson of the U.S.

He split the Soviet defense and collected the loose puck, then fired it into the open goal, tying the game with one second left in the period. With confusion in the arena, the Soviet team returned to their locker room. They then had to send out three players and a goalie to take the faceoff and run off that final second of the period.

In the second, Tretiak was pulled and replaced by the Soviets' backup, Vladimir Myshkin. Later on, the Soviet coach would describe this decision as the biggest mistake of his career, as it changed the course of the game. The Soviets outshot the Americans 12-2 in the second period, but each team managed to score a goal, meaning that the U.S. was behind 3-2 heading into the third period.

For the first six and a half minutes in the third period, the United States had not managed to get a single shot on goal against Myshkin. In fact, over 27 minutes of hockey, the Soviets had only allowed two shots. Then, a slashing penalty was called against Vladimir Krutov, putting the U.S. on the power play. During the special teams play, Mike Ramsey put a shot on goal, then U.S. captain Mike Eruzione missed a chance wide. Dave Silk brought the puck into the zone once more, but when he was knocked down, the puck slid over to Mark Pavelich, who used the broken play opportunity to take a shot on goal, catching the Soviet goalie off guard just long enough to allow the puck to slide under his pads and into the net, tying the game.

Then, a couple of minutes later, the U.S. got another chance when Pavelich passed the puck to Eruzione in the slot, who fired another shot past Myshkin. The Soviet goalie did not track the shot, as he was screened by one of his own players. The Americans had the lead with ten minutes left in the game.

What followed is what many American players would call the "longest ten minutes of their lives." The Soviet team increased the intensity of their attacks, hitting the goalpost on a shot just moments after the go-ahead goal. Coach Brooks tried to keep his players calm and focused, and he told them to stay on the game plan. Instead of playing too conservatively, the Americans continued to play on offense when opportunities arose.

Surprisingly, as the time ticked down, the Soviets never pulled their goaltender for an extra attacker. As it turned out, the Soviet coach did not believe in the technique, so they never used it when they needed a tying goal. With a couple more great saves from Craig, the U.S. team was able to run out the clock and secure the 4-3 victory.

It was not the gold medal game, but it certainly felt that way for the Americans. They had defeated the favorites, giving them a chance to win the gold with one more victory. The game was deemed the 'Miracle on Ice', as Ken Dryden, former goaltender of the Montreal Canadiens, delivered his now-famous line of commentary as the final seconds expired: "Do you believe in miracles? YES!"

The U.S. team would go on to defeat Finland to win the gold medal, and they were also behind in that game before coming back to victory. In the future, 13 of Team USA's 20 players would go on to have careers in the NHL, though only five of them played more than 500 games in the league. Though the team did not consist of NHL stars, they pulled off what most could not and defeated one of the best international teams to ever play the game.

Did You Know?

1. The American team also beat the Russian squad 20 years prior enroute to the 1960 Olympic gold medal.

2. Herb Brooks, coach of the 1980 team, was the last player cut from that 1960 team that also won gold.

3. Jim Craig played the arcade game Centipede with Russian player Sergei Makarov the night before the game. The two players were friendly but could only communicate by smiling and nodding.

4. The American players tried singing "God Bless America" after their win, but they didn't know all the words.

5. Coach Brooks helped the 2002 team to a silver medal but passed away in a car accident one year later.

6. The Lake Placid ice rink was renamed the Herb Brooks Arena in honor of Brooks and his accomplishments in that building.

CHAPTER 9:

TIGER WOODS AT THE 1997 MASTERS

No one in the golf world saw it coming. The best moments in sports' history often come out of nowhere, when no one is expecting it. That moment of surprise, shock, wonder, and awe can stick with a sports fan for generations. That moment for many golf fans came in 1997 when Tiger Woods competed in the Masters Tournament.

Tiger Woods was 21 years old and had won three PGA Tour events. Analysts and pundits were interested to see how he fared during his first major tournament as a professional golfer because, after all, he had missed the Masters cut one year earlier, when he had competed as an amateur. Many expected a better performance, but how much better could he really be after one year?

The golf world respects Augusta National Golf Club so much that they'll tell you it takes years to learn and understand how to play the course effectively. Because of that, it only made sense that Tiger would have to be patient and fail some more before he could learn to win.

There was one golfer on the Tour who knew that Tiger had what it took to win, and his name was Mark O'Meara. But why was he so sure? Well, the Friday before the Masters, Mark and Tiger played a friendly round together at Isleworth, one of the toughest courses in Florida. Tiger shot a 59, making very few mistakes and rarely missing a putt. O'Meara was impressed, then he went to the same course with Tiger the next morning. This time, they were playing for money. Ten dollars per hole.

On number ten, the first hole they played, Tiger birdied and went one-up on O'Meara. When they got to 11, Tiger hit a hole-in-one. O'Meara gave Tiger a hundred dollars and went home. He knew that Tiger was prepared for the Masters from the firsthand experience of getting beaten two days in a row.

While Tiger played well at a different course with no one watching, tackling the Masters Tournament is a different monster altogether. When Tiger teed off with Nick Faldo, the defending champion of the tournament, his front nine did not go well. His first tee shot missed the fairway quite badly, and he bogeyed the first hole. By the end of his first nine holes, he was +4. Four bogeys, zero birdies.

It was a far cry from the performance he had conducted a week prior. In positions like these, some players lose the tension in their shoulders and relax, withdrawing from the pressure to play average golf. Tiger Woods did not let go of his round. Instead, he tried to recall what his golf game had felt like when he shot 59. Heading to the back nine, he found that feeling.

Tiger birdied number ten, then a par on 11. Refusing to back down, he fired birdies on 12 and 13 before burying an eagle on 15. For good measure, he birdied 17, finishing his round at -2.

Tiger Woods was three shots back from the lead, but the entire clubhouse of golfers knew that Tiger had just put everyone on notice.

On Friday, the second round began as Tiger teed off with Paul Azinger, another veteran of the Tour. Tiger's front nine was much improved from the day before, as he shot -2 with three birdies and a bogey. On the back nine, it was more dominant. After four steady pars, he eagled 13, followed by birdies on 14 and 15 to shoot a -4 on the back. In total, the round was -6 for a total of -8.

At the halfway point of the tournament, Tiger was leading by three shots over Colin Montgomerie. The cuts were made, reducing the field and increasing the pressure on the remaining golfers. Would young Tiger Woods be able to withstand the pressure and capture his first major championship?

It was Tiger's third round that put the tournament out of reach. In terms of dominant golf, it was one of the best rounds ever played. He opened with a par on the first, then birdied the second hole, just as he had done on Friday. He made two more pars, then a birdie on number five. A par on number six, then two more birdies on seven and eight. Through the front nine, it was another -4 added to his score, putting him at -12 for the tournament.

It was a score good enough to keep the rest of the field from ever approaching him, but he continued to play his game of golf. Tiger then played the back nine with no substantial errors. Zero bogeys, and three more birdies, including the par-5 15th, which Tiger had played well all week. At the end of the round, he was -15 for the tournament, and the next closest competitor was -6.

The Masters record for the largest margin of victory was nine shots. Jack Nicklaus set the record in 1965, and he needed four rounds to build that lead. Tiger had matched it in three! Of course, he could underperform on Sunday, but the odds of that happening seemed slim.

Tiger's final round was not perfect, as winds around the course picked up and wreaked havoc on golf balls flying. Still, he did enough to grow his lead, gaining five birdies to go against his two bogeys. Tiger's final score for the four rounds was -18, and Tom Kite was in second place on the weekend, with a -6.

It was not the greatest margin of victory for any major championship, but Tiger would get that record later in his career.

If you're a fan of golf, then you likely know what happened next with Tiger Woods. He would not let this tournament be a one-hit wonder, and he would not be satisfied with just one major victory. To date, Tiger is still actively competing on the PGA Tour, though his last major championship victory was in 2019. Over those 22 years of golf, Tiger has won a lot of golf tournaments.

In fact, Tiger Woods has won 82 PGA Tour events, which is tied for first place all-time. He is also third on the all-time list of European Tour wins with 41. He would go on to win the Masters tournament four more times, while he would win the PGA Championship four times, the U.S. Open three times, and The Open Championship three times. Overall, his 15 major championship victories are second on the all-time list.

Over his career, he was named the PGA Player of the Year ten times, the PGA Tour Player of the Year 11 times, and he was even awarded the Presidential Medal of Freedom in 2019 for his accomplishments in golf.

One of the measurements demonstrating how much Tiger Woods contributed to the sport over the past couple of decades is evident in his 1997 Masters win. For his victory, Tiger was awarded a cash prize of $486,000. Most recently, Jon Rahm of Spain won the tournament, and his prize money was $3,240,000.

Tiger Woods brought new eyes to the sport with his dominance, and also with the emotion and anger he would often show on the course. Whenever he made a big putt on the green, he would yell with the crowd around him, often pumping his fist to release some of the adrenaline he had built up in his veins.

But Tiger did more for the game than just bring emotion and new eyes. He also showed players on the Tour that there was a great benefit to exercising, lifting weights, and being in good shape for the game. He could hit the ball further than almost all of his contemporaries for a few years after he entered the Tour, and players had to adapt to his skillset.

Tiger Woods showed the world a new way to play and enjoy the game of golf. He changed how golfers approached the game, how fans appreciated the golfers, and how sponsors could bring money into the sport for everyone's benefit. The 1997 Masters Tournament results caught the golf world off guard, but there was no surprise when the incredible Tiger Woods continued to dominate for the next 15 years.

Did You Know?

1. Tiger Woods is at the top of the all-time money list with nearly $121 million in winnings.

2. Woods was the number one golfer in the world rankings for a record 683 weeks. Greg Norman is second with 331 weeks.

3. From Tiger's first professional round of golf, it took him 291 days to become the top-ranked player in the Official World Golf Ranking.

4. Tiger Woods has made three holes-in-one as a professional, and 17 more in his career.

5. Tiger is the only player to have won eight times at a single course, and he's done it at three different courses: Torrey Pines, Bay Hill, and Firestone.

6. Tiger Woods is the only player to win all four majors in a row, though he did not win them all in the same year.

CHAPTER 10:

JACKIE ROBINSON BREAKS THE COLOR BARRIER IN THE MLB

When discussing American sports, it is important to recognize that, although many were established after the Civil War, when slavery had been ended, cultural change was slow and painful. Due to this, it was always an important moment when a Black person helped push that change forward. Sports served as an important catalyst, and professional baseball, which was the most popular sport in the country, was the most important of them all.

On April 15, 1947, Jackie Robinson broke the color barrier in Major League Baseball when he played first base for the Brooklyn Dodgers. How he got to that point in his career, and the effect it had on American culture, are the truly incredible aspects of this story. Let's examine both.

As a young man growing up in California, Robinson's family lived in poverty compared to the community around him. Because he and his friends were often not allowed to participate in any recreational events, Robinson briefly joined a neighborhood gang but quickly decided to abandon the idea. As he began his high school days, Robinson played several varsity sports, including track, baseball, football, and basketball. He also excelled in tennis, where he won a singles championship in the Pacific Negro Coast Tennis Tournament.

After Robinson finished his high school studies, he enrolled at Pasadena Junior College, where he continued playing several sports, though he gave up tennis. He did break a junior college record in the broad jump, with a jump of 25 feet and 6.5 inches.

Though his sports career seemed to be on a good track, he was starting to react strongly when he encountered racism. This was a good thing, to be sure, but it was also risky. Robinson was arrested in January 1938 for disputing another Black student's detention. He received a two-year suspended sentence, but it also left Robinson with a reputation.

Still, Robinson continued with his studies and his athletics, moving on to the University of California Los Angeles (UCLA) after his time at Pasadena had finished. While there, he became the first athlete in school history to earn letters in four sports: football, basketball, baseball, and track. During his time on the football field, he set the school record for rushing yards per carry in a season, with 12.2.

He even won the 1940 NCAA Championship in the long jump event.

Actually, baseball was Robinson's worst sport, in comparison. During his only season on the diamond for UCLA, his batting average was a dismal .097.

Robinson left UCLA before graduating, taking a job with the National Youth Administration until the government ended that organization a year later. In the meantime, Robinson began to pursue dreams of playing professional football, as he spent time with the Honolulu Bears, a semi-professional team, and the Los Angeles Bulldogs of the Pacific Coast Football League.

All of that came to an end when Japan attacked the United States at Pearl Harbor, dragging the country into World War II. Interestingly enough, Robinson's refusal to allow any racially charged decisions from authority figures may have saved his life. After he received his commission from the Officer Candidate School, he was moved from Fort Riley in Kansas to Fort Hood,

Texas, where he got into an altercation with an Army bus driver who had told Robinson to move to the back of the bus.

Robinson refused, and when he arrived at his destination and left the bus, he was arrested by military police. Robinson's commander refused to court-martial him, so he was transferred to another battalion with a commander who was willing to charge him with multiple offenses. All of this delayed, permanently, his deployment overseas. Robinson ended up being acquitted of all charges by an all-White panel of officers, and he never saw combat before he was honorably discharged in November 1944.

After leaving the military, Robinson briefly rejoined the Los Angeles Bulldogs before accepting an athletic director position at Samuel Huston College in Austin, Texas, which meant he would coach the men's basketball team, as well. The team struggled to attract players, but Robinson still earned respect from the school and teams around the conference.

Then, an invitation to play baseball arrived. The Kansas City Monarchs of the Negro leagues offered to pay Robinson $400 per month to join the team. Robinson enjoyed success on the field, but he hated the league itself, as it was unorganized and seemed to cater to several different gambling interests. While Robinson was playing for the Monarchs, he began looking for opportunities to join an MLB team, beginning with a tryout for the Boston Red Sox. Unfortunately, the event turned out to be a humiliation and a waste of time.

Four months later, a more serious opportunity came his way when the Brooklyn Dodgers asked to interview Robinson. The team's management was worried that if Robinson was added to their organization, he might blow up at a comment from an opponent or spectator, leading to a terrible, possibly violent situation.

Robinson began to understand that if he wanted to play professional baseball in America, he would have to keep his cool when someone said or did something terrible to him. He would have to put up with a lot of abuse to be the first Black player in the modern game.

After being assured that Robinson would be able to rise above the racism, the Dodgers offered him a contract of $600 per month, and he was set to join the Dodgers' minor league team, the Montreal Royals, in 1946. The Royals manager did not want Robinson, but the signing went ahead all the same.

Beginning with his first spring training, which took place in Florida, where segregation was still being forced, things were uncomfortable for Robinson. He could not practice at certain facilities, as they refused to let Black players inside.

The organization had to meet with local officials in Daytona Beach to allow Robinson to make his team debut in March 1946, when the Royals played against the Brooklyn Dodgers, their parent team. It marked the first time a Black player on a minor league team played against a major league team since the 1880s.

One month later, Robinson made his official minor league debut against the Jersey City Giants. During his first at-bat, the Giants' catcher demanded that his pitcher hit Robinson with a pitch. However, the pitcher was Warren Sandel, who had played against Robinson when they both lived in California. Sandel refused to hit Robinson, who grounded out.

While his first minor league at-bat was unsuccessful, he finished his first game four-for-five, and his first hit was a three-run home run. By the end of the International League season, Robinson finished with a .349 batting average and was named the league MVP. More importantly, fans in Montreal were supportive of Robinson. However, he continued to face hostile people during road trips.

One thing was clear: whether the fans loved or hated him, they showed up to watch him play. The International League saw their attendance increase substantially for games involving Robinson. Pairing his strong performance with the increase in attendance, it was only a matter of time before he would be called up. In fact, six days before the beginning of the 1947 season, Robinson got the call. Wearing number 42, Jackie Robinson debuted with the Dodgers for a preseason game on April 11, 1947. The rest of Robinson's story is history, but his journey to Major League Baseball shows what an incredible man he was. He had to endure what so many minorities had to endure during that time, but he did it as a focal point of American culture.

His baseball career ended up being quite successful, a far cry from his dismal year of college baseball. Robinson was named an All-Star six times, and he was named the National League MVP once in 1949. He won one World Series with the Dodgers, in 1955, before he stepped away from the sport in 1956. While the team only won a single World Series, his ten years of play brought the Dodgers to the World Series six times.

Jackie Robinson did not have the longest MLB career, but his presence on the diamond might have had the biggest impact on the history of the sport. His participation effectively ended a 60-

year-long practice of segregation in professional baseball, opening the door for many more talented minorities to find their paths to the league.

Robinson was elected to the Baseball Hall of Fame as a first-ballot candidate, even after he instructed voters to focus on his baseball accomplishments and not his cultural impact. But these things cannot be separated. Sports mimic the competition and intensity of life, and Robinson's impact on both have been crucial to American culture. His incredible career will continue to be celebrated for decades to come.

Did You Know?

1. Larry Doby was the first African American player in the American League, and he was close friends with Robinson.

2. Robinson traveled on a speaking tour through the Southern United States during the baseball offseason, earning him more money for those speaking engagements than his baseball contracts brought in.

3. He retired from baseball to take a job with Chock Full O' Nuts, an American coffee company.

4. Robinson also became the first African American sports analyst.

5. Robinson's number 42 was retired by the entire league in 1997.

6. On April 15 every year, all MLB players wear 42 on their jerseys to honor Jackie Robinson Day.

CHAPTER 11:

BRANDI CHASTAIN'S WINNING PENALTY

It can take a special moment for an unpopular sport to capture the attention of an entire country and birth renewed interest in the game. Often, sports like this require superstars to bring more eyes to the game, helping it grow and mature in the culture of their homeland. However, women's soccer in the United States struggled to gain footing in their early days, despite international success.

The 1999 FIFA Women's World Cup took place during the summer of 1999 across eight different cities across the United States. It was only the third time ever that women's international teams had competed in this tournament, with the previous two taking place in 1991 and 1995.

With the game being played in their home country, the United States team knew that this was their opportunity to show their country how great they were, how great the game was, and how much potential there was to invest in the sport.

It was also the first time that there would be 16 teams competing, an increase from 12 in the previous iteration of the tournament. More teams meant more competition - and more chances for failure.

The pressure on the US team was intense, but they benefited from a favorable group draw when they were grouped with Nigeria, North Korea, and Denmark, all of which were considered weaker international teams at the time.

The US team opened the tournament in front of 78,000 fans in New York, where they defeated Denmark 3-0 on goals from Mia Hamm, Julie Foudy, and Kristine Lilly. Five days later, the team played in front of 65,080 spectators, who thought they might be seeing a dramatic collapse. In the second minute of their match against Nigeria, the US team conceded a goal to Nkiru Okosieme after a defensive miscue.

In the 19th minute, the team got some fortunate help when Ifeanyichukwu Chiejine scored an own goal to even the score. It had taken a little while, and the home team fans had to endure a little bit of uncertainty, but the own goal shifted the momentum for good. One minute later, Mia Hamm scored, followed by goals from Milbrett, Lilly, Akers, and Parlow, giving the US squad a 6-1 lead at halftime. They would add one later in the match for a 7-1 final score.

To complete the group stage, the Americans played against North Korea for 50,484 fans in Massachusetts. This match was much closer, as the North Koreans excelled defensively, keeping the US players off the scoresheet in the first half. The Americans finally broke through in the 56th minute, followed by goals in the 68th and 76th minutes, securing the Group A victory.

Nigeria advanced with the United States to the knockout stage, along with Germany, Brazil, Norway, Sweden, China, and Russia.

In the quarterfinals, the United States faced a tough opponent in Germany, and it didn't help when they conceded a goal five minutes into the match. Defender Brandi Chastain put the ball into her own goal, giving the German team an early lead. The Americans equalized 11 minutes later, but Germany regained the lead in stoppage time before half.

In the second half, the Americans refocused, and Chastain put the ball in the correct goal in the 49th minute to equalize a second time. Then, a goal in the 66th minute from Joy Fawcett put the Americans ahead for good, sending them to the semifinals.

Brazil and the United States squared off on US Independence Day to determine the finalists of the tournament. The Americans struck quickly, as Cynthia Parlow capitalized on a mistake from the Brazilian goalkeeper to head the ball into the goal. The Brazilians spent the rest of the match trying to even the score, forcing Briana Scurry to make several important saves to maintain the lead. The Americans added a penalty kick goal in the 80th minute to seal the victory.

On the other side of the bracket, a strong China squad flattened Norway with a five-goal victory.

In front of a record 90,185 spectators, the Americans and the Chinese faced off for the title, a rematch of the 1996 Summer Olympics, where the US team had prevailed, 2-1. The two teams played a closely contested match, with both teams trading opportunities. The Americans had more chances, but they could not find the back of the net.

As the game moved into extra time, China had two quality chances that were spoiled by Scurry and midfielder Kristine Lilly. With no scoring at the end of extra time, the 1999 Women's World Cup would be decided by a penalty shootout.

Xie Huilin opened the scoring for Team China, and Carla Overbeck answered for the Americans in the first round. Qiu Haiyan scored in the second round, as did Joy Fawcett.

For the third round of shooters, Liu Ying's attempt was saved by goalkeeper Briana Scurry. There was some speculation, though, that Scurry had left her line prematurely, and that the save should have been called back. Scurry dismissed these allegations later on, stating that it was how goaltenders played the game.

Kristine Lilly put the Americans ahead by scoring her penalty kick. Zhang Ouying scored to even the score briefly, before Mia Hamm scored to put the Americans ahead once more.

In the fifth and potentially final round of shooters, Sun Wen scored to tie the score at 4-4, leaving Brandi Chastain with an opportunity to win the tournament for the United States. Four months earlier, as it so happened, Chastain had a penalty kick against this same China team during the Algarve Cup competition. She had missed that penalty.

With all of that pressure, and with the memory of her recent missed penalty still fresh in her mind, Brandi Chastain walked to the penalty spot for her chance at glory. As she struck the ball to her right, the Chinese goaltender dove in the right direction. However, Chastain's shot had too much pace and was too well-placed for the shorter Chinese keeper to reach. As the ball ripped into the netting and sealed the World Cup for the US, Chastain spun around and ripped off her jersey, exposing her sports bra to the crowd as she cheered along with the 90,000 fans in attendance.

The image of Brandi Chastain gripping her jersey in one hand as she screamed in joy for her team's victory would become an iconic image for women's sports in the United States, as fans around the world saw a woman celebrating without fear or shame of reprisal.

Not only was it a gigantic step forward for women's soccer, but it was also a monumental step forward for women's rights around the world. The quality of soccer demonstrated by those women's teams was much improved, and the Final between those two strong teams helped to validate the sport. Chastain's celebration, which some would have scoffed at or been offended by, was a symbol of women gaining respect and support from sports fans all around the world.

The United States team, with the victory, became the first women's team to capture a second World Cup, and they would go on to win the tournament twice more. With their four victories, the American team holds more championships than any other international women's team.

The victory also helped supporters and organizers begin discussions to create a professional league for women's soccer in North America. While the attempt lasted a few years before falling apart in 2003, it helped lay the groundwork for the current iteration of the league, the National Women's Soccer League, which formed in 2012 and has been running ever since.

Did You Know?

1. Sissi of Brazil and Sun Wen of China tied for most goals scored, with seven.

2. The 1999 Women's World Cup was the first to feature 16 teams, an increase from 12.

3. Because of its success with fans, the United States also hosted the 2003 Women's World Cup.

4. 123 goals were scored at the tournament, averaging over three goals per match.

5. Total attendance for the tournament was 1.21 million people.

6. Instead of building new stadiums, the host country utilized American football stadiums for the matches.

CHAPTER 12:

THE RUMBLE IN THE JUNGLE

There are many iconic moments in the world of boxing, but there are few that give birth to a new style of fighting. There are also even fewer that have taken place in an African country. This chapter examines the cultural impact of The Rumble in the Jungle, a boxing match in October 1974 between two of the greatest fighters to ever put on the gloves: George Foreman and Muhammad Ali.

Muhammad Ali had been the undisputed heavyweight champion up until 1967 when his title was taken away from him after he refused to be drafted by the U.S. Army. He waited three and a half years before he could return to the ring, then quickly worked his way up the rankings once more to try and win his title back from the champion, Joe Frazier. Ali made it back to the top but lost to Frazier by a unanimous decision.

This sent Ali back down the rankings, and he had to patiently take fights until he could get another shot at Frazier, or anyone else who might take the belts from him. As it happened, up-and-coming George Foreman defeated Frazier in January 1973, becoming the undisputed heavyweight champion. Foreman and Ali, though competitive, did not want to fight unless it was for the five million dollars as promised by promoter Don King.

However, King did not have the money, nor could he host such an event in the United States, so he began to look abroad. As it happened, he had a connection to the dictator of Zaire, Mobutu Sese Seko, who agreed to host the match. The funds were collected by the dictator of Libya, Muammar Gaddafi, though his methods were never made public.

Still, the fight was set, and the two fighters would be facing off in front of 60,000 people. George Foreman, the undisputed champion, was coming into the match with several advantages. He was nearly seven years younger than his opponent, and his reach was one inch longer. He also had the pedigree of being undefeated to that point in his career, with 40 wins and zero losses. Of those 40 victories, 37 of them were by knockout, and he was considered to have one of the strongest punches in the history of boxing.

Muhammad Ali, coming into the fight as the challenger, had a record of 44 wins and two losses. His 44 victories included 31 knockouts, and although he was not known for his power, his speed and footwork were considered legendary. He was a great defender, and his punching combinations were often too fast for his opponents to counter.

The two fighters each had their strengths, but Foreman was considered the favorite, and Ali was the underdog by a four-to-one margin. With the boxing world excited about these two titans meeting for the title, Don King arranged for the bout to be shown on closed-circuit television in movie theaters all over the United States, while it was to be broadcast over-air all around the world.

Though the fight was originally scheduled for September 24, the match was delayed when Foreman was unintentionally cut over his eye by his trainer. Because the cut required 11 stitches, the match was pushed back five weeks to allow Foreman to recover. The new date was set for October 30, and both fighters arrived months ahead of time to acclimatize to the weather, particularly the humidity.

With everything set in place, the world was ready for these two titans to meet. What happened in the fight would go down in boxing history.

In the first round, Ali used an aggressive technique to disorient Foreman. Ali was using his right-hand jab to attack Foreman's head, all while not setting his left hand. The speed was too much for Foreman, but the punches from Ali were not hurting him either.

Going into the second round, Ali unleashed his secret weapon, his counter to Foreman's haymaker-throwing style. As Foreman approached his opponent, Ali backed up against the ropes and covered up, allowing Foreman to punch at Ali's body and arms, dodging any other attack by leaning back into the ropes to extend the distance between them.

As Foreman was expending energy to throw heavy punches, Ali's defense allowed him to deflect or dodge attacks entirely. He would occasionally jab at Foreman's head, but he would otherwise wait against the ropes, hoping the Foreman would tire himself out at some point. This defensive strategy was new to the world of boxing, and Ali would later name it the "rope-a-dope" technique.

After many rounds of Ali's technique, Foreman began to tire, and the quicker punches from Ali began to take their toll. Near the end of the fifth round, Ali staggered Foreman with a quick combination, even though it had seemed that Foreman was in control for the rest of the round.

Even worse for Foreman, Muhammad Ali was not being hurt by his punches. Foreman thought he was making headway against his opponent, but he realized that Ali was mostly unharmed when he heard Ali taunting him in the middle of the fight.

"They told me you could punch!"

"That all you got, George?"

Part of Ali's fame had come from his trash talk ability, and he was using it to his advantage against Foreman.

Into the eighth round, Ali began his counterattack, landing right hook after right hook, culminating in in a five-punch combination that snapped Foreman's head back. Then, a hard right to Foreman's exposed face sent him to the mat. Foreman was able to get back up to one knee, but the referee called the fight before he could finish getting up.

George Foreman had lost the fight, but there were some accusations of cheating that were never truly investigated, or even taken seriously. First, Foreman accused Ali's manager of loosening the ropes around the ring, allowing Ali to lean back farther, taking more power away from Foreman's attacks. Foreman also said that his water had been drugged, that it tasted like medicine and made him feel dizzy and lethargic.

The only accusation Foreman made that was truly debunked was when he said that the referee had counted him out too quickly. Video of the event showed that he had been on the mat for more than 11 seconds.

Ali was the upset victor, and although the two boxers understood the gravity of the moment, they were both interested in a rematch. When Foreman lost another fight in 1977, though, he decided to retire instead of seeking a rematch with Ali.

A few years later, the two boxers became friends. A documentary film called *When We Were Kings* was released in 1996, documenting the story behind the fight, the fight itself, the cultural impact, and more. It took the film's creator more than 20 years to finish editing it, but the film won the Academy Award for Best Documentary Feature that year, 1996.

Muhammad Ali and George Foreman had a fight in a new venue that was broadcast around the world. Millions of people witnessed the two best boxers fight in a long, arduous match. They watched first-hand as Ali introduced a new defensive strategy, one that would influence the sport for decades to come. Most importantly, the fight created a new friendship between the two combatants, which helped strengthen the cultural impact of the incredible moment.

Did You Know?

1. Analysts estimated that the bout was watched by one billion people worldwide.

2. Both Foreman and Ali utilized orthodox boxing stances.

3. The fighters would only sign a contract for the fight if the purse was $5 million.

4. Boxer Joe Frazier gave color commentary for the fight.

5. All of the undercard fights were altered after the rescheduling of the main event.

6. The estimated gross revenue for the closed caption broadcast at the time of the fight was $100 million.

CHAPTER 13:

THE CUBS BREAK THE CURSE

This incredible baseball story begins with a tavern owner and his pet goat. You read that right. Sometimes, sports stories talk about the G.O.A.T., the Greatest of All Time in any sport, but this is an actual goat we're talking about. With real fur and everything. This particular goat, named Murphy, plays a role in one of the most iconic curses ever bestowed upon a professional sports team.

Here is Murphy's story. Actually, it is the story of the Chicago Cubs and their 100-plus years without a World Series victory.

The scene is the 1945 World Series. The Detroit Tigers and the Chicago Cubs are facing off for the championship, and the Cubs are leading the series two games to one. Game 4 is underway at Wrigley Field in Chicago, the Cubs' first home game of the World Series. If they win Game 4, they'll have a commanding lead in the Series, being only one game away from sealing the championship.

Fans in Chicago were excited for their team, as they had not won a World Series since 1908. Though they had not won since 1908, they had been to the championship series six times from 1908 to 1945 with zero victories. Perhaps this time the team will be lucky, those fans hoped.

With a lead in the series and a chance to win two home games for the championship, the odds were in their favor until a certain fan with his pet goat decided against it.

William Sianis was the owner of the Billy Goat Tavern, and his pet goat was the mascot of his tavern. Because Sianis was doing well with his tavern, he was able to afford box seats for the World Series, and he brought his goat along with him, likely to gain attention and advertising for his business.

Even though Sianis had that box seat, separate from the rest of the fans in the stadium, he was kicked out of the stadium with his goat because of how much the goat smelled. Not taking this turn of events very well, Sianis allegedly declared, as he was leaving the stadium, that "Them Cubs, they ain't gonna win no more." Other reports allege that Sianis sent a telegram to the owner of the Cubs with a similar statement: "You are never going to win a World Series again because you insulted my goat."

The Cubs would go on to lose the 1945 World Series to the Detroit Tigers, in a thrilling seven-game series. Over the next 71 years, the Chicago Cubs would undergo a whole lot of losing. With each season of failure, the team's fans would remember the curse from William Sianis, and the legend would grow in importance.

Fans began looking for signs of the curse whenever the team had particularly poor luck during their decades of losing. During a 1969 game against the Mets, as both teams were competing for the NL East pennant, a black cat found its way onto the field and walked by the Cubs dugout. Since black cats are considered unlucky, fans attributed the cat's appearance to the curse, as the Cubs would go on to lose that series with the Mets, who went on to win the NL East and the World Series later that season.

The curse even seemed to affect other teams. The infamous error by Bill Buckner while he was a member of the Boston Red Sox was connected to the Cubs. Buckner missed a routine ground ball in the tenth inning of Game 6 of the 1986 World Series, allowing the Mets to score the winning run. The Mets tied the series and won in Game 7. Buckner played seven seasons with the Cubs before being traded to the Red Sox, and he had allegedly been wearing a Cubs batting glove under his glove when he made the error.

Then, of course, there was the infamous moment involving a fan by the name of Steve Bartman. The year was 2003. The Cubs were up 3-2 in the National League Championship Series against the Florida Marlins. In the eighth inning, the Cubs were leading 3-0, and they had already retired one Marlin, leaving them five outs away from a trip to the World Series. Marlins batter Luis Castillo hits a ball that was going foul, and Cubs outfielder Moises Alou was running toward the side barrier for a potential catch.

As the ball descended, several fans reached over the barrier for the chance to catch a souvenir. The unlucky fan to catch the ball was Steve Bartman. As he caught the ball, Alou's glove was waiting just under his hands. Bartman had a souvenir, but he had cost the Cubs an out. The curse was in effect once again. The Cubs still needed two outs in the eighth, but they gave up eight runs and lost the game, 8-3. They lost in Game 7, and 1945 remained the last time the Cubs had reached the World Series.

It had become a running joke in the league, funny to all baseball fans - except those who loved the Cubs. The New York Mets joked that their sweep of the Cubs in the 2015 NLCS was because their second baseman, Daniel Murphy, was a connection to the goat that figured in the original curse.

After decades of the Chicago Cubs trying, but failing, to win a championship and break the curse, including many outlandish attempts from fans attempting to help break it, they had their best chance during the 2016 season. The Cubs finished the regular season with 103 wins, eclipsing 100 wins for the first time since 1935.

It took the Cubs six games to dispatch the Los Angeles Dodgers in the NLCS, giving them their first trip to the World Series since 1945. As it turns out, the day of that game, October 16, 2016, was the 45th anniversary of Willian Sianis's death. It was a huge step toward breaking the curse, but the Cleveland Indians stood between the Cubs and a return to glory. If Game 1 was any indication, the Cubs were not much closer to breaking the curse. The Indians took full control of the game, winning by a convincing 6-0 score.

The Cubs, to their credit, bounced back in Game 2, winning 5-1 and evening out the series as it shifted from Cleveland to Chicago.

With the series tied and the team playing their first World Series game in Chicago since 1945, the Cubs came out and lost. In a close 1-0 game, the Cubs were shut out in front of their home fans, falling behind 2-1 in the series. To make things worse, the Cubs also lost Game 4, 7-2. At this point, they were down three games to one, and the Indians only needed one more game to win the World Series and send the Cubs back to their miserable curse. But the Cubs proved that their curse was wearing off. In Game 5, the team won a close game, 3-2, closing the gap between them and the Indians. In Game 6, back in Cleveland, the Cubs stormed to a 9-3 victory, forcing a decisive Game 7.

The Cubs jumped out to a quick lead with a run in the top of the first inning, but the Indians answered back in the bottom of the third with a run of their own. The Cubs scored twice in the fourth, taking a 3-1 lead. Both teams scored twice in the fifth, making the score 5-3 in favor of the Cubs. Chicago added one more run in the sixth inning, giving them a three-run lead.

Things were looking good for the Cubs. They didn't allow a run in the bottom of the sixth, and the bottom of the seventh also kept the Indians with only three runs on the scoreboard. However, when the bottom of the eighth rolled around, the Indians found their offense, including a two-run home run that tied the game.

Going into the ninth with a tied game, the Cubs had a great chance to score after advancing a runner to third base. However, they botched a squeeze bunt and then grounded out to end the threat. Then, Cubs pitcher Aroldis Chapman retired the three Indians batters to end the ninth.

After a short rain delay, the teams returned to the field for the tenth inning, the World Series championship hanging in the balance. Ben Zobrist, after going 0-for-4 for the rest of the game, hit an RBI double to give the Cubs the lead. Then, Miguel Montero, batting .091 during the playoffs, hit an RBI single to give the Cubs a two-run lead going into the bottom of the tenth.

Pitcher Carl Edwards Jr. earned the first two outs for the Cubs, putting them one out away from breaking the curse. Then, he walked one Cleveland batter, who advanced to second base without a challenge. Then, Rajai Davis hit an RBI single to bring the Indians to within one run. The tying run was at first base, and the winning run was at the plate. With their pitcher struggling, the Cubs opted to bring in another pitcher. However, nerves were high for fans when Mike Montgomery came to the mound. The Cubs were one out from the championship, and they brought in a pitcher who had never registered a save in his career.

Thankfully for the Cubs, Michael Martinez grounded out. The Chicago Cubs won the World Series and officially broke their curse. It took the team 108 years to win the championship once more, ending more than a century of pain for baseball fans in their city. The incredible story of the curse made their pain more entertaining for them and for all baseball fans.

Did You Know?

1. Sianis tried to lift the curse before he passed away, but it did not seem to work.

2. The Harry Caray Restaurant in Chicago tried to break the curse by electrocuting the baseball touched by Steve Bartman.

3. Someone even butchered a goat and hung it from the Harry Caray statue in 2007, in another failed attempt to break the curse.

4. The 1989 movie *Back to the Future Part II* depicted the Cubs winning the World Series in 2015.

5. The Cubs' 103 wins was their best season since 1910.

6. Ben Zobrist was named MVP of the series.

CHAPTER 14:

THE PERFECT DOLPHINS

There are few NFL records more respected, celebrated, and desired than that of the perfect season. It can be difficult to believe that only one team in NFL history achieved such a feat, but that distinction belongs to the 1972 Miami Dolphins. That special, incredible team won every game during the regular season and playoffs, finishing the year 17-0, including a victory in the Super Bowl. From today's perspective, it might feel easy to imagine a high-flying offense with a passing attack that was nearly unstoppable, a quarterback who was agile and accurate, and defenders who were constantly looking for interceptions and sacks.

The truth behind this team is that their brand of football was quite different from today's game, though they were still dominant in many aspects of the game. Let's examine how this magical team came together and made history with an incredible season.

The Miami Dolphins franchise entered competition in 1966 as part of the American Football League, where they competed until the end of the 1969 season. Then, following a merger with the NFL, the Dolphins became a member of the AFC East and the American Football Conference beginning with the 1970 season. It only took the Dolphins one season to rise to the top of the AFC, winning the conference in 1971 and laying the groundwork for what was set to follow in 1972. In fact, only a loss in the Super Bowl to the Dallas Cowboys had stopped Miami from becoming champions sooner. As it turned out, they still needed a few more wins to put them over the top.

They had a future Hall of Fame coach in Don Shula, an All-Pro quarterback in Bob Griese, another All-Pro in Larry Csonka, who played running back, and for good measure, a second All-Pro running back in Mercury Morris. Between those three players on offense, with Don Shula running the show, it was expected for the Dolphins to contend again for the 1972 season, just as they had the previous year.

There are other important names, though, that were important to the team's success. One anecdote came from running back Larry Csonka, who met a big lineman at, of all places, a car dealership. Larry Little was working for a car dealership in Miami, Florida during the summer of 1968 when Csonka came in to buy a car. Csonka was a rookie that year with the Dolphins, but he could tell that Little was a strong individual. He lobbied the team's front office, asking them to acquire Little as soon as possible. After all, as a running back, Csonka had a vested interest in the strength of the linemen, as it would help his performance. Still, as a rookie, it was quite brave of Csonka to stick his neck out for a specific player. The Dolphins traded for Little, adding him to the line and bolstering Miami's running game and pass blocking.

Another important connection was the backup quarterback position, which Don Shula filled with someone he'd worked with in the past. During his time with the Baltimore Colts, Shula had become quite familiar with Earl Morrall, a veteran quarterback who had lots of success during the regular season but had not performed very well in the postseason with limited opportunities. Morrall was often the backup, including bench time behind the legendary Johnny Unitas. Shula knew that Morrall could help the team, but no one could have predicted just how much help he would be.

To open the season, the Dolphins traveled to Kansas City for a contest against the Chiefs. The Chiefs had lost to the Dolphins in the playoffs the season before, but it was a close game that ended in double overtime. This season, though, the Dolphins were ready. They were leading 17-0 at halftime, cruising to a comfortable 20-10 victory. Out of 296 yards of offense, only 100 came from passing.

In Week 2, the Dolphins played the Houston Oilers, once again jumping out to a comfortable halftime lead and keeping their advantage to secure another victory. Csonka, Morris, and Griese each had one rushing touchdown in the effort.

Week 3 featured the first real test for the team, as they traveled to Minnesota to face the Vikings. At the end of the first half, Miami trailed 7-0. In the third quarter, they collected a pair of field goals from Garo Yepremian. Minnesota scored another touchdown early in the fourth quarter, making the score 14-6. But, with a 51-yard field goal, followed by a Griese touchdown pass to Jim Mandich, the Dolphins clawed back to win 16-14.

Week 4 featured another halftime lead for the Dolphins over the Jets, leading to a ten-point victory. Then, in Week 5, disaster struck the team when Bob Griese went down with an injury. Backup Earl Morrall came into the game, completing eight passes out of ten attempts. Two of his passes were touchdowns, though he only totaled 86 yards on his completions. Still, the Dolphins won comfortably against the Chargers.

Griese's injury was a serious one, and it did not appear as though he would be able to return for the rest of the season. The team had to rely on their running game, and occasional throws from Morrall, if they wanted to continue their winning ways.

In Week 6, with Morrall under center, the Dolphins fell behind 13-6 at halftime thanks to an interception from Morrall that was returned for a touchdown. In the second half, Csonka and Morris added rushing touchdowns to help pull ahead. The Buffalo Bills scored a touchdown to get within one, instead of going for two and the tie. Miami held on to win, 24-23.

Relying mostly on the rushing attack, Miami's defense played decisively in Week 7, as the Dolphins shut out the Baltimore Colts 23-0. Week 8 was another victory, of course, but it also featured a rough outing for Morrall, who was 5-for-14 and 89 yards. It became apparent throughout the season that Miami's rushing attack and defense would be crucial for victory.

Week 9 was a blowout victory against a weak New England Patriots team, 52-0. Their Week 10 opponent, the New York Jets with Joe Namath at quarterback, put up a much tougher fight. The Dolphins trailed 17-14 at halftime, and the teams both traded touchdowns after halftime with Miami getting the only score of the fourth quarter, taking a 28-24 lead and holding on for the victory.

Comfortable victories over the Cardinals, Patriots, Giants, and Colts brought the Miami Dolphins to 14-0, ending the regular season with a perfect record. Even better, Bob Griese was back and ready to play again. Would the Dolphins turn back to him full-time for the playoffs, or stick with Morrall, who helped the team get nine of their 14 wins? Also, imagine the pressure entering the playoffs as the overwhelming favorite. If a team finishes the regular season undefeated, anything less than a Super Bowl victory would be considered a wasted effort. The Dolphins had a lot on their shoulders as the playoffs began.

In the Divisional Round, the Dolphins hosted the Cleveland Browns, and they decided to put Morrall under center. The Dolphins got on the board first with a blocked punt returned for a touchdown, and a field goal before the end of the first quarter gave them a 10-0 lead.

After a scoreless second quarter, the Browns scored a touchdown in the third. Miami added a field goal to start the fourth quarter, but the Browns added another touchdown, taking a 14-13 lead halfway through the final frame. The Dolphins were able to score another touchdown to go ahead for good, as Jim Kiick ran it in from eight yards out. The Dolphins' defense stifled the Steelers in the AFC Championship, keeping the team ahead by double digits for most of the fourth quarter. After notching two late interceptions against quarterback Terry Bradshaw, the Dolphins allowed one touchdown in the final few minutes, but it wasn't enough. The Dolphins were 16-0 on the season and on their way to the Super Bowl. The Washington Redskins were favored to win, but only by one point. Even though Washington had three losses in the regular season, they were considered the stronger team. Miami wasn't deterred, and the game quickly evolved into a defensive battle. Miami decided to start Griese over Morrall for the final game, which helped with how tight the game was played. The Dolphins got on the board with a 28-yard Griese pass to Howard Twilley, and Kiick added another rushing score in the second quarter, giving the perfect Dolphins a 14-0 lead at halftime.

However, the Dolphins would not score again, leaving it up to their defense to secure the victory. The defense, for their part, played perfectly, a reflection of their record. The special team's unit blundered in the fourth quarter, giving up a fumble return for a touchdown. Still, the Dolphins were able to hold on and win 14-7.

A perfect season concluded with a Super Bowl championship, a feat unmatched in professional football. Even with their backup quarterback, the Miami Dolphins found a way to win. Only the New England Patriots have come close, winning 18 games before losing in the Super Bowl. Players from the '72 Dolphins celebrated the Patriots' loss, clinging onto their record and celebrating their unique place in football history. It was an incredible feat, one that will likely remain unmatched for a long time.

Did You Know?

1. The Dolphins led the league on offense and defense.

2. Nine players from the roster were named to the Pro Bowl that year.

3. There were also four AP All-Pro players on the team.

4. Running backs Csonka and Morris were the first teammates to both rush for 1,000 yards in a season.

5. The '34 Bears, '42 Bears, and '07 Patriots have all finished the regular season undefeated, but they all lost their championship games.

6. Larry Little would go on to enter the Hall of Fame.

CHAPTER 15:

ANNIKA SORENSTAM

The game of golf is yet another where men and women compete separately, as men often drive the ball farther and require longer courses for an appropriate challenge. However, a few women have broken that line and competed directly with the men. One of those special competitors is Annika Sorenstam.

From a young age, it was clear that Annika had a talent for athletics. She had become a nationally ranked junior tennis player in her home country of Sweden. She was also a talented skier, so much so that the coach of the country's national team asked that she and her family move to a better skiing area to develop her skills on a year-round basis! The family did not make that move, though, and instead focused on golf.

The family played together, and Annika had to share a set of clubs with her younger sister. Annika would use the odd-numbered clubs in the bag, and her sister would use the even numbers. As a young, new player, her first established handicap was 54.

When Annika began to compete at the junior level, she realized that if she ever won a tournament, she would have to give a victory speech. She was a very shy person, so she determined that it was better to intentionally lose at the last moment. When tournament organizers realized what she was doing, they changed the rules and made it so both the winner and runner-up would have to give a speech.

Since Annika couldn't avoid the speech either way, she decided that winning was better than intentionally losing. From there, her golf career blossomed.

During her time as an amateur, Annika had a highlight victory at St Andrews, where she won the St Rule Trophy, an international amateur tournament. She also played for the Swedish National Team from ages 17 to 22. She also won tournaments on the Swedish Golf Tour in 1990 and 1991 before moving to the United States.

While attending the University of Arizona, Annika Sorenstam became the first non-American to win the individual college Division I Championship. She was also the first college freshman to win the title, though she was older than most college freshmen in the United States.

Her efforts at Arizona helped her qualify for the U.S. Women's Open in 1992, where she made the cut and finished tied for 63rd. Despite Sorenstam's promise as an emerging golfer, she did not earn an LPGA Tour card during her first year as a professional, as she was one shot short of the card at her final qualifying tournament. As such, she had to compete on the Ladies European Tour for the 1993 season.

While her first season couldn't be on the LPGA, Sorenstam excelled overseas, earning Rookie of the Year honors on the European Tour. She was also invited to three LPGA tournaments, and she played well on those occasions, earning over $47,000 and two top-ten finishes.

Sorenstam was able to qualify for the LPGA Tour with a T-28 finish at the LPGA Final Qualifying Tournament, but she did not notch a win during the 1994 season. However, with three top-ten finishes, one of them at the Women's British Open, she won LPGA Rookie of the Year.

In her second LPGA season, Sorenstam proved that she was only getting started. In July 1995, Sorenstam won her first LPGA Tour event, and it also happened to be a major championship. She won the U.S. Women's Open by one stroke. She went on to win two more tournaments that year, along with finishing first on the Tour's money list for the season. It was a dominant campaign, but she was determined to continue winning.

Sorenstam won the U.S. Women's Open for the second year in a row, and then she added two more wins in 1996. What followed was a golf career that many consider to be one of the best in women's golf history.

Sorenstam would go on to win ten LPGA major championships, including three of the U.S. Women's Open, three Women's PGA Championships, three Chevron Championships, and one Women's British Open. Her 72 LPGA Tour victories puts her third on the all-time list behind Kathy Whitworth and Mickey Wright. Those ten majors are tied for fourth on the all-time list, as well, behind Patty Berg, Mickey Wright, and Louise Suggs. In the modern era of women's golf, Sorenstam was by far the best to play the game.

She was so good, in fact, that she was invited to play an event on the men's Tour. Babe Zaharias had made the cut 58 years before Annika played a Tour event, but Annika was the next woman to ever attempt the feat.

However, while today's culture is more accepting of women in sport, many golfers on the PGA Tour at the time were against Sorenstam's appearance. Vijay Singh, one of the best golfers of the 90s, was vocal about this. He told the press that he considered it a sideshow and that she would not be able to compete.

Women golfers were apprehensive, as well. They worried that if Sorenstam did not perform well, it would send a message that women golfers were not skilled or talented. In short, it could damage their sport.

Other golfers were more supportive. Tiger Woods even suggested that she be allowed to play several events with the men, to give her a chance to become more acclimatized with the length of the courses. Annika's round with the men came in 2003, at the Bank of America Colonial in Fort Worth, Texas. She was the top-ranked female player at the time, and she was dominating the Women's Tour. When she arrived at the course, the media buzz was electric.

The pressure on her must have been immense, but if her play was any indication, she was able to handle it. In her first round she showed off her excellent accuracy. She hit 13 of 14 fairways, and she also hit 14 greens in regulation. She finished her first round with a +1 score, due to a three-putt on 18.

Still, it was an impressive round. Sorenstam would shoot +3 the following day and miss the cut by those three shots, but she had not disappointed the golfing world. She proved that women could play at high levels, and she kept up with the men when it came to distance and power off the tee.

It was historic, even if it was not a Cinderella moment.

Even more impressive, for a man or a woman, is that Sorenstam holds the record with the lowest round ever recorded in professional women's competition. Starting on the back nine of Moon Valley Country Club, Sorenstam was beginning her second round of the 2001 Standard Register Ping Tournament. When asked what she was thinking and feeling during her round, she said that she wasn't thinking about much. She was just focused on hitting fairways and greens.

Whatever was going on for Sorenstam that day, it worked for her. She birdied each of her first eight holes. By the end of the round, she had a -13 on the scorecard for a 59. With that score, she is the only woman to ever break 60 in a single round of golf. That record may fall one day, as there are men who have shot 58, but her accomplishment is likely to keep her at the top of the list for quite a long time.

Annika's decorated career not only put her at the top of women's golf, but her accolades were also good enough to create a bridge connecting the men's and women's games. She collected many trophies and awards, and her earnings still have her at the top of the women's career money list, even though she stopped playing in 2008. She was voted Player of the Year eight times, a number that is also an LPGA record.

Annika Sorenstam dominated women's golf for a decade, and she made it a better sport in the process.

Did You Know?

1. Sorenstam was the first LPGA player to play a season with a scoring average under 70.

2. She has a share of the LPGA record for the biggest comeback win. She erased a ten-shot deficit to win a tournament in 2001.

3. She won the Mizuno Classic five times in a row, which is an LPGA record, of course.

4. At the age of 33, Sorenstam was inducted into the World Golf Hall of Fame.

5. She holds the record for the lowest scoring average for a season with 68.6969.

6. She represented Team Europe in the Solheim Cup for eight of those events.

CHAPTER 16:

BOBBY THOMSON AND THE SHOT HEARD 'ROUND THE WORLD

Few plays in professional baseball are famous around the world, and even fewer of them have a title assigned to them afterward, much like a historical moment. This chapter is going to examine one such event that took place way back in 1951, between two baseball teams that were being watched by fans and enthusiasts all over the world.

The "Shot Heard 'Round the World" might sound familiar to those who have studied American history, as it is the name given to the first rifle fired during the American Revolutionary War. While this moment in baseball is not as historically important to the country, some might argue that its cultural impact is greater, as baseball was the top sport in the country for more than a century.

Either way, this moment was truly spectacular, and it deserves its own chapter.

In 1951, the teams that finished on top of the two leagues, the American League and National League, automatically qualified to compete in the World Series. There were no playoffs with multiple teams. There were no Wild Card games. The two teams at the top of the standings went straight to the World Series. This greatly increased the drama of the regular season, especially near the end as teams jockeyed for the best record.

During this period of professional baseball, three teams were contending for the National League pennant: the Philadelphia Phillies, Brooklyn Dodgers, and New York Giants. The Dodgers opened up a 13.5-game lead with about 50 games left in the season, and it looked likely that they would advance to the World Series, where the New York Yankees also enjoyed a sizable lead in the American League.

The Philadelphia Phillies were unable to keep pace, but the New York Giants were getting hot at the right time. From August 12 to 27, 1951, the Giants won 16 games in a row, leaving them only six games back from the Dodgers.

Four weeks later, the Dodgers had a 4.5-game lead, but there were only ten days left in the season. That final stretch was quite incredible, as the Dodgers lost six of their final ten games. The Giants, on the other hand, finished the season on a seven-game winning streak. After the dust had settled, the Dodgers and the Giants were tied with identical records of 96 wins and 58 losses.

At that time, instead of looking to statistics to break the tie, or a single-game, winner-take-all playoff, the National League used a three-game playoff system to determine who would go to the World Series. After the Dodgers won the coin toss, they had the choice to play Game 1 at home or on the road, with the remaining two games played at the other location. The Dodgers picked their home turf for the first game, but this backfired when they lost 3-1.

The Dodgers responded, though, defeating the Giants 10-0 to set up the deciding Game 3. With over 34,000 fans watching in the stadium, and for the first time in American history, the game was being broadcast across the country on NBC.

So, with all the cards on the table, it's time to discuss the New York Giants' third baseman, Bobby Thomson. Few players who have participated in such a historic, monumental game have had such a significant impact on its result. However, not all of his effects on the game were positive for his team.

After the Dodgers scored a run in the first inning to take the lead, the Giants had a chance to respond in the second inning.

With Whitey Lockman on first, Thomson was up and hit a line drive to left field. Wanting to stretch his hit into a double, he went for second but didn't notice that Lockman had not advanced. Thomson was tagged out at second, stalling his team's attempt at tying the game.

However, five innings later, with the score still 1-0 in favor of the Dodgers, Thomson had another opportunity to help his team. Monte Irvin opened the bottom of the seventh with a double to left field, and Lockman then advanced him to third with a sacrifice bunt. Thomson came up and hit a sacrifice fly to deep center field, scoring Irvin and tying the game.

Then, in the top of the eighth inning, disaster struck for Thomson and the Giants. After getting the first out, Pee Wee Reese and Duke Snyder both reached on singles. With runners at the corners, Jackie Robinson was at the plate when a wild pitch allowed Reese to score. The Dodgers had restored their lead, but the inning wasn't over.

The Giants elected to walk Robinson, giving them another opportunity for a double play to end the inning. However, Andy Pafko hit a ball toward Thomson at third base, who couldn't make the catch. Snider scored on the play, and the Dodgers were up 3-1.

The Giants registered another out when Gil Hodges popped out to third, where Thomson made the play. However, the very next batter, Billy Cox, hit a ground ball through Thomson that made it out to left field, scoring Robinson and giving the Dodgers a 4-1 lead going into the bottom of the eighth. While Thomson was not assessed on any errors during the inning, he certainly didn't make the most efficient plays possible, either.

Things were looking even worse for the Giants when they were retired without a hit to finish the eighth. Into the top of the ninth, Larry Jansen came on to pitch. In nine pitches, he retired all three Dodgers batters, sending the game to the bottom of the ninth.

With their season on the line, the Giants were desperate to find some last-second offense. On the mound for the Dodgers was the same pitcher that had been there for the entire game, Don Newcombe. Al Dark opened the inning with a single to first, then Don Mueller singled to right field, and Dark advanced to third. With runners on the corners, Monte Irvin popped out, putting the Giants two outs away from the end of their season.

Whitey Lockman stepped into the batter's box and doubled to left, scoring Dark and sending Mueller to third base.

The score was 4-2 in favor of the Dodgers, and Bobby Thomson was up to bat. It was his opportunity to make up for the issues he could have prevented earlier in the day. For the Dodgers, they decided to bring in a fresh pitcher. Ralph Branca was on the mound, hoping to get two more outs and move on to the World Series.

The first pitch was a strike. The second pitch, though, was a line drive to left from Thomson. Although it was not hit very high in the air, the ball cleared the fence, and the stadium exploded in cheers as the Giants had won the game.

Jackie Robinson, well known for breaking the color barrier in the MLB, made sure to watch Thomson round the bases in case he missed one to cause an out and extend the game. After the celebrations for the Giants, though, Robinson and a few of his teammates visited the Giants' locker room to congratulate them on their victory.

The Giants would go on to lose the World Series to the Yankees in six games, but the incredible ending to that National League playoff series was the story that endured from that season. Bobby Thomson hit a home run so dramatic that it has been etched into the history of the game.

Did You Know?

1. Many American soldiers stationed in Korea were able to listen to this game on the radio, adding to its lore.

2. The Giants' comeback during the season, culminating with the home run, is known as "The Miracle of Coogan's Bluff."

3. Russ Hodges delivered the most iconic broadcasting call of the play, though other broadcasters thought his call was unprofessional.

4. The only reason a copy of Hodges' call survived the times was that one fan, Lawrence Goldberg, asked his mom to tape-record it because he had to work.

5. The Dodgers' bullpen coach resigned a couple of months later, though he denies it was his idea to bring Branca to the mound in the ninth.

6. Years later, rumors of sign stealing by the Giants began to come forward. Giants players confirmed a telescope was used to observe and steal signs from the Giants' clubhouse, and then a buzzer wire communicated to the dugout what kind of pitch was coming.

CHAPTER 17:

CAVALIERS COME BACK AGAINST THE WARRIORS

In the history of the NBA, there are few things more secure than a three-to-one lead in the NBA Finals. It is a lead that is nearly impossible to overcome. In fact, before the 2016 NBA Finals, it was impossible. This chapter examines that series and why it is so incredible. Much of the story surrounds one player, LeBron James, who many consider to be the best player to ever walk onto the court.

Let's start with his situation with the Cleveland Cavaliers because those details make this story so much more special.

LeBron James was drafted way back in 2003, with the first pick, by Cleveland. He had grown up in Ohio, so he was essentially picked by his hometown team. Unlike other first-round picks, James had a ton of media attention leading up to the draft, because many scouts and analysts considered him to be a generational talent.

He lived up to that reputation within a year or two of entering the league. He was determined to bring a championship to Cleveland, Ohio, a city, and state that had gone through quite a bit of losing in recent history, and not just on the basketball court. The city wasn't getting much help from the rest of their sports franchises, either.

Unfortunately, after seven seasons with the Cavaliers, the team had only reached the NBA Finals once, where they were swept by the San Antonio Spurs. LeBron James was unhappy in Cleveland, so he accepted a deal to play in Miami, where he helped the Heat win two championships. Still, James was unsatisfied that he had left Cleveland without a title, so he went back in 2014.

In his first season back with Cleveland, he helped the team reach the NBA Finals, where they were defeated by the Golden State Warriors, a team working to establish a dynasty behind two of the best perimeter shooters to ever play the game, Stephen Curry and Klay Thompson.

Undeterred by their recent failure, LeBron and the Cavaliers reached the NBA Finals once more after defeating the Toronto Raptors in six games. On the other side of the bracket, the defending champion Golden State Warriors, led by Stephen Curry, defeated the Oklahoma City Thunder in seven games.

It was a rematch of epic proportions, and few analysts gave the Cavaliers a chance, especially considering the outcome of the 2015 Finals. The Warriors were looking to establish their dynasty with a second-straight championship, and since not much had changed from the previous year, it was looking likely. It helped that the Warriors broke the NBA record for regular season wins, with 73.

Still, the series had to be played. The first two games took place on the Warriors' home court, and they held their advantage by winning those first two games. The Warriors won Game 1 by 15 points, then they followed it up with a 33-point victory in Game 2.

Only three teams had ever come back from a 2-0 deficit in the NBA Finals. The 2005–06 Miami Heat managed the feat, as did the 1976–77 Trail Blazers and the 1968–69 Boston Celtics. It was not a good situation for James and the Cavaliers.

However, Cleveland proved that they could hang with the Warriors and that they could stop Curry and Thompson from scoring at will, with a 30-point victory of their own in Game 3.

They had won a big game on home court, putting them only one game down in the series. Another home win would tie the series, but it was not meant to be. The Warriors responded, winning by 11 and gaining a 3-1 lead.

While three teams had found their way back from a 2-0 deficit, a 3-1 hole was a different matter entirely. To this point in NBA Finals history, it had never been done. Any team up 3-1 in the Finals went on to win the NBA Championship. Now, you read the title, and you know that Cleveland found a way to do it. But how?

Game 5 was a win of sheer will from LeBron James and his All-Star teammate, Kyrie Irving. For the first time in NBA Finals history, those two players became the first teammates to both score 40 or more points in the same game. It also helped that Draymond Green of the Warriors, one of their best defenders, had to serve a suspension for Game 5 due to receiving his fourth flagrant foul of the playoffs in Game 4. Also, sadly, Andrew Bogut, center for the Warriors, injured his left knee and would not return in the series.

The final score of Game 5 was 112-97, putting the series at 3-2 for the Warriors. However, Game 6 would take place in Cleveland, giving them a bit of an advantage as they tried to even the series.

Game 6 featured another 40+ point performance from LeBron James, including 18 straight points for his team to begin the fourth quarter, but Tristan Thompson of the Cavaliers stepped up, registering a double-double by the end of the first half. Irving added 23 points for the Cavaliers, while Draymond Green, back from his suspension, was limited to eight points. Stephen Curry fouled out, which was the first time the league MVP fouled out in the NBA Finals since the year 2000, when Shaquille O'Neal last did it.

With the win, the Cavaliers became the third team in NBA history to reach Game 7 after trailing 3-1 in the series, though the next step would still be the hardest. Even worse for the Cavaliers, the final game would be taking place on the Warriors' court.

Unlike the rest of the series that featured wide margins of victory, Game 7 was a tense, close matchup. There was a total of 20 lead changes, and the game was tied 11 different times. At half, the Cavaliers were trailing 49-42, but the last 4:39 of the game featured zero points from the Warriors. One of the biggest moments in those final minutes is now known as "The Block." With the score tied at 89 points each and less than two minutes left on the clock, Irving missed a floater that was rebounded by Andre Iguodala, who began to run up the floor with Stephen Curry. J.R. Smith was the only defender back, allowing the two Warriors players to pass the ball twice before Iguodala went up for a layup, which was mildly contested by Smith.

As the passes were being made, LeBron James was racing back up the court to catch Iguodala. Thanks to Smith contesting the shot, causing Iguodala to tuck the ball for a moment before releasing it, James was able to close the gap, time his jump, and smack Iguodala's shot against the backboard and away from the rim. The Cavaliers had the ball back, but the game was still tied. With each team missing shots on another possession, Kyrie Irving hit a three-point shot over Stephen Curry to give the Cavaliers a lead with only 53 seconds remaining. Curry missed a three-point shot of his own on the next possession, and James was fouled while driving to the basket on the ensuing drive.

James made one of the two free throws, sealing the game for the Cavaliers, as the Warriors tried two more three-point shots as the final seconds ticked away.

The game was over, and history was made. It was an incredible moment within an incredibly close game, all within an amazing, classic series between two of the best teams and the biggest All-Stars in the game. The Cleveland Cavaliers had brought a championship to a city that hadn't had a major sports champion since the Browns won the NFL championship in 1964.

During the next season, though, the Warriors would get their revenge as the two teams met once more in the NBA Finals, winning the series 4-1. Then, in the 2018 Finals, the two teams would meet once more, with the Warriors sweeping the Cavaliers. After that second straight Finals loss, LeBron James would move on from Cleveland once more, this time to Los Angeles. Neither the Lakers nor the Cavaliers have been back to the Finals since then.

Did You Know?

1. Both Leandro Barbosa and Tristan Thompson shot over .630 from the floor during the series.

2. This Finals represented the 14th time in NBA history that the series was a rematch from the previous season.

3. LeBron James received all 11 Finals MVP votes for his performance in the series.

4. James became the first player in NBA history to lead a series in points, assists, rebounds, blocks, and steals.

5. The Warriors won their first 24 games to start the season.

6. The Warriors were the first team to ever make more than 1,000 three-pointers in a season.

CHAPTER 18:

SERENA WILLIAMS

Few players in the tennis world have dominated the game as long as Serena Williams. She broke several records in both singles and doubles, forever changing the game. More importantly, she showed that women can compete at high levels for long periods, despite injuries, form slumps, and a pregnancy.

Let's jump into Serena's incredible story and how she changed the game of tennis forever.

As a child, Serena was the youngest of five girls, with three older half-sisters and her older sister Venus. At a young age, her family moved from Saginaw, Michigan to Compton, California, which is where Serena began to play tennis at the age of four. Her father, Richard, homeschooled Serena and her sister, Venus. He also taught them to play tennis.

After a few years of practice, the family moved to West Palm Beach, Florida, allowing the sisters to attend a tennis academy run by Rick Macci, a Master Professional in the Professional Tennis Association. With more coaching, Serena began to compete in national junior tennis tournaments. However, at the age of ten, Serena's father began to slow down on tennis practice and competition. He said he wanted his girls to focus on school, but his decision was also influenced by instances of racism from parents of other players.

When she slowed down on her tennis schedule, Serena was the top-ranked tennis junior tour player under ten years old in Florida. A couple of years later, Serena's father pulled her from Rick Macci's tennis academy to coach her by himself. While the move was considered unusual, it worked for the Williams family.

Serena was anxious to begin her professional career but was denied entry into the Bank of the West Classic in 1995 because she was only 14. She was able to enter the Bell Challenge later in the year with a wild-card entry that allowed her to get around the age restriction. She lost in the opening round and didn't enter another tournament for over a year.

While it was a rough, unorthodox start to her career, it didn't take too long for things to shift in Serena's favor. During the 1997 season, she lost in the opening round of three straight tournaments before winning her first main-draw match at the Ameritech Cup Chicago. She defeated the seventh- and fourth-ranked players, becoming the lowest-ranked player to beat two opponents ranked in the top ten in the same tournament.

While she lost in the semifinals of that tournament, her ranking went from 304 to 99.

In her 1998 season, Serena reached the quarterfinals of seven tournaments, but no further. In mixed doubles, she won titles at Wimbledon and the US Open, sharing the other two titles with her sister for a "family" slam. By the end of the year, she was ranked 20th in singles competition.

After scoring her first Tier I title in 1999, Serena went on a tear at the U.S. Open. She defeated Kim Clijsters, Conchita Martinez, Monica Seles, Lindsay Davenport, and Martina Hingis to win. She became the first African American woman since 1958 to win a Grand Slam tournament. At the end of her second year on the tour, she was ranked fourth in the world.

Williams won two tournaments in 2000, ending the year ranked number six. She and her sister, Venus, won gold medals at the Olympic Games that summer.

In 2001, the Williams family faced controversy when Serena won the Pacific Life Open. The crowd was unhappy that the Williams family appeared to be giving Serena a significant advantage. In the semifinals of that tournament, Serena and Venus were scheduled to face each other, but Venus withdrew with an injury. This gave Serena the victory and a lot of rest for the final.

As a result of the accusations, neither sister returned to that tournament for 14 years.

Serena and her sister would next win the Australian Open Doubles Grand Slam, but 2002 was when Serena turned the corner on her career.

After having to withdraw from the Australian Open in 2002 due to injury, Serena returned with a vengeance. Serena won the year's other three Grand Slam events, earning the top spot in the women's rankings for the first time on July 8, 2002. In each of those Grand Slam victories, she had to defeat her older sister in the finals. The tennis world had been fully taken over by these two spectacular women, but Serena was the clear-cut number one.

She would win the Australian Open the next year, in 2003, completing the Career Grand Slam, also known as the Serena Slam, as she won all four tournaments in a row, though not in the same year.

Over her career, Serena Williams used her powerful two-handed backhand shot to win 73 career titles, which is fifth on the all-time list. She won 23 Grand Slam singles titles, second on the all-time list, behind only Margaret Court. Besides her two-handed backhand, Serena was also well known for having one of the most powerful serves ever seen in the women's game. Not only was it very fast, but it was also terribly accurate. On record, she has the third-fastest serve in women's tennis history.

Another aspect of Serena's serve that was so respected by her opponents was her ball toss. It was the same motion every time, meaning that the opponent would not be able to tell where she was planning to hit the ball. Her motion was the same, but the ball would travel to different places on the court.

With her groundstrokes, Serena kept her stance open, which allowed her to hit the ball at sharper angles, creating more difficulty for opponents trying to return them. The forehand shot she utilized created a lot of topspin, which accelerates the ball when it hits the ground.

She preferred to play on the baseline, though she was capable of coming to the net when necessary to finish points. With her aggressive offense and excellent defensive skills, Serena would hit a winner when no one in the arena thought it was possible!

With all those wins, Serena accumulated over $94 million in winnings, which is more than double the second player earner, Venus Williams.

What was special about her time at the top of the tennis world was how often she was able to persevere through trials and injuries. Several times, she had to miss parts of the tennis season due to an injury, often to her knees. Many times over, analysts of the game would incorrectly predict her downfall, only for her to rise back to the top and prove them all wrong.

If Serena had a negative side to her, it was that her temper could get the best of her. She was fined by the WTA on several occasions for racket abuse, as well as comments made to umpires and ball runners. After one particularly nasty incident in which Serena was called for a foot fault on a serve, she threatened the lineswoman, saying she would shove a tennis ball down her throat.

Because it happened at a Grand Slam, the committee considered suspending her from next year's event but instead fined her $175,000 and placed her on probation. She had to behave properly for two years at the Grand Slam events to avoid suspension. She apologized for her outburst after initially refusing to do so.

Still, Serena's impact on the game has been a whole lot more good than bad. She inspired young children of color across the United States to pick up the game, and a few of those inspired kids are now on the tour. She changed the way women were viewed on the court, as she used raw power to win many games and matches during her career. Serena's incredible run will not be matched anytime soon.

Did You Know?

1. Serena won one gold medal in tennis singles, and three golds in doubles.

2. She is the only player, male or female, to complete the Career Golden Slam three times.

3. Of all professional sports, Serena is the highest-earning female athlete of all time.

4. Serena and Venus lost a Battle of the Sexes match against 203rd-ranked Karsten Braasch in 2003.

5. Serena is part of an investors' group that owns Angel City FC, a team in the National Women's Soccer League.

6. Williams served as Ambassador for the Purple Purse Project, a foundation to financially help victims of domestic abuse.

CHAPTER 19:

MICHAEL PHELPS

Have you ever been told that you can be the best at something, as long as you keep trying? When you were told that, depending on how old you were when you heard it, you probably thought "the best" meant that you'd be better than the other kids in your class, or better than your sports opponents from around the region. It's unlikely that you sat back and thought, "I can be the best in the entire world!"

It's hard to wrap your head around an idea like that. Fortunately for us, there's one Olympic athlete who rises above the rest, showing us that being the best in the world is possible. Michael Phelps is that Olympic athlete, and his accomplishments demonstrate that being the best in the world can be achieved with an incredible work ethic and belief in yourself. Let's look at the story of the best swimmer of all time.

Michael Phelps was born in Baltimore, Maryland, to parents who worked as a middle school principal and state trooper. His father played college football and tried out for an NFL team but did not make the squad, so there were some athletic genes passed down.

At seven years old, Michael learned to swim, and he and his sisters fell in love with the sport and continued to pursue it. He caught on quickly, as he captured the national record for his age group in the 100-meter butterfly. He was only ten years old at the time.

He captured several more age group records that have lasted for many years since.

When he turned 11, he began training with a coach named Bob Bowman, who himself was a swimmer at Arizona State University in the mid-1980s. Bowman was very disciplined in his training, keeping to a very tight and detailed schedule. Phelps took to it immediately, and it began to pay off. At the age of 15 years old, Michael Phelps qualified for the 2000 Summer Olympics in Sydney, Australia. He was the youngest male to make the American swim team since Ralph Flanagan in 1932. At those games, Phelps finished fifth in the world in the 200-meter butterfly event.

He didn't win a medal that year, but to be the fifth best in the world at the age of 15 is still impressive. He made it to the final of that event, which is more than any 15-year-old could dream of doing.

Continuing to train with Bowman, Phelps was not ready to slow down. At the 2001 World Championships, Michael Phelps captured his first World Record, in the 200-meter butterfly, capturing gold at the event in the process. With his world record, at 15 years and nine months, he became the youngest athlete ever to break a world record in a swimming event. He was more than a year younger than the previous record holder, Ian Thorpe, who had been 16 years and ten months at the time of his world record swim.

What followed was a whirlwind of medals and world records. At the 2002 Pan Pacific Championships, Phelps captured three golds and two silvers, and one world record in the 4x100-meter medley.

At the 2003 World Championships, it was four golds, two silvers, and three world records.

As the 2004 Olympics approached, much of the competitive swimming world knew what was going to happen. Michael

Phelps captured six gold medals and two bronze medals. He broke two world records, three Olympic records, and two national records.

At the end of the 2004 Olympics, Phelps had become the second male swimmer to win more than two titles in individual events, as Mark Spitz had also won four back in 1972.

Some athletes, after a spectacular show at the Olympics, might decide to call it a career and move on. Some of them lose motivation and want to put their efforts into something else. Michael Phelps was not satisfied.

At the 2007 World Championships, Phelps won seven gold medals, breaking five world records in the process. It was truly an incredible scene. Every swimmer around the world knew this man's name, and they knew he was going to be the best once again when the 2008 Olympics arrived.

Michael Phelps arrived at the 2008 Olympics in Beijing with the world watching and hoping to see history take place. The world knew that he was going for eight gold medals, but the odds were astronomical. Surely, no one could do that, right?

Just to make sure the world knew he was capable, he won gold in the 400-meter individual medley, shattering the world record by almost two full seconds.

Then, in the 4x100 freestyle relay, Phelps and his teammates had a close call in one of the most exciting races in Olympic sports history. Alain Bernard of the French team had the lead in the final leg of the race, and Jason Lezak of the United States was desperately trying to catch him as Phelps watched from the edge of the pool, already done with his leg.

For the first half-lap, it looked as though Lezak would not be able to close the gap, but in the final 25 meters, Bernard could not keep Lezak from getting closer. Phelps and his teammates became more animated on the edge, watching and yelling encouragement as the two swimmers raced to the end of the pool. As both competitors reached out to touch the wall, there was a slight pause in Phelps' reaction.

The finish had been so close that it was impossible to tell with the naked eye who had touched first. Thanks to the technology in the walls of the pool, the computer knew. When it showed the United States had won by eight hundredths of a second. The team exploded in cheers, hugging, and celebrating.

Phelps had won his second gold medal, but more importantly, he showed his character to the world. Bernard of the French team had been quite vocal before the race about being ready to crush the Americans, but Phelps didn't hold it against him. After the initial celebration, Phelps went to console his opponent, showing grace that few could have had in that moment.

Still, he had work to do. He continued his winning ways with a world record in the 200-meter freestyle and his third gold medal, making him only the fifth Olympic athlete to ever win nine golds.

The very next day, he sought to blow them out of the water. Despite his goggles filling with water, leaving him unable to see for the final 100 meters, Phelps set another world record and won his fourth gold of the Olympics in the 200-meter butterfly. With his tenth gold, he was already at the top of the list, alone, for individual gold medals won by any athlete.

Less than one hour later, Phelps helped the U.S. 4x200-meter freestyle team win another gold medal and set another world record. Two days later, Phelps collected his sixth gold medal of the 2008 Games with a world record time in the 200-meter individual medley. His closest opponent was more than two seconds behind.

Then, Milorad Cavic of Serbia made headlines when he said that it would be a good thing if Phelps lost one race. He said this, of course, because he was the main opponent for the next race in Phelps' gauntlet. The 100-meter butterfly was up next, and it did not begin well for Michael.

Off the start, he trailed Cavic immediately. In the 50-second race, Phelps struggled to gain any ground on his opponent, but in the last ten meters, he began to close the gap. Even as the two swimmers stretched for the final touch on the wall, it looked as though Cavic had won. Then, miraculously, the results showed that Phelps had won by one hundredth of a second (0.01).

It was truly a remarkable moment in a series of remarkable performances. The stars seemed to be aligning for Phelps, who had seven golds, tied with Mark Spitz for the most gold medals at a single Olympic Games.

But Phelps had one race to go. It was his chance to win an unprecedented eighth gold.

He was swimming the third leg of the 400-meter medley, but he would be swimming the butterfly of the medley, arguably his strongest style. When it was his turn to swim, his team was behind both Australia and Japan. Then, Michael Phelps did what only Michael Phelps could do. With a time of 50.1 seconds, he turned in the fastest-ever butterfly split, which gave his teammate a lead of more than a half second. That turned out to be the difference, as the Americans went on to win another gold medal, Phelps' eighth.

It was a stand-out achievement in the history of sports. Michael Phelps established himself as the best swimmer in the world, not only of that time, but *all time*. No one will be able to duplicate what he did at those Olympic Games.

Actually, there is one person who thinks it can be done, and that is Michael Phelps. He has stated that records are always there to be broken and that anyone can accomplish something great if they set themselves on a path to achieve it.

Between the 2012 and 2016 Olympics, Phelps collected nine more gold medals. His total gold medal count from the Olympics stands at 23, and the next closest competitor on the list has nine.

He dominated the world of swimming from 2004 to 2016 before retiring from swimming. His incredible performance will likely live on for generations to come, until another brave swimmer believes in themselves enough, and pushes themselves hard enough to achieve the unthinkable.

Did You Know?

1. Michael Phelps' wingspan is three inches longer than his height.

2. Phelps' foundation helps to promote water safety and swimming lessons.

3. Michael was diagnosed with attention deficit hyperactivity disorder at the age of six.

4. Many questioned if Phelps was cheating during the 2008 Olympics. He passed all nine of the drug tests he was given during the Games.

5. A video game with Michael's name on the title was released in 2011 to mixed reviews.

6. Phelps has the world record for the longest televised golf putt, at 159 feet.

CHAPTER 20:

THE RED SOX COMPLETE THE COMEBACK

In professional hockey, basketball, and baseball, the playoff series require that one team win four games against their opponent to advance. If one team loses the first three games of their playoff series, the odds are astronomically against them coming back to win. Erasing a 3-0 deficit has happened a handful of times in hockey history, and it has never happened in basketball history. However, baseball history has only one such event, when a team trailed 3-0 and tried to come back.

This chapter focuses on the 2004 American League Championship Series between the New York Yankees and the Boston Red Sox. It was a rematch of the 2003 ALCS, when the Yankees defeated the Red Sox in the bottom of the 11th inning in Game 7 with a walk-off home run.

The two teams were very evenly matched, just as they had been for the past two years. Over those two seasons, the teams had played each other 45 times. Boston won 23, New York won 22. The Red Sox had won eight of 11 games during the 2004 season, but many of the games were very close. Eight of the games were decided by either team's final at-bat. Scoring between the two squads in those games was almost dead even, with Boston scoring 106 runs to New York's 105.

History was on the Yankees' side, though. The two teams had met in this scenario four other times in MLB history, with the winner going to the World Series. In those four matchups, the Yankees won each time.

In Game 1, Curt Schilling started for the Red Sox. He was newly acquired for the 2004 season, as the Red Sox hoped he could help the team get by the Yankees this time around. However, Schilling had suffered an injury during the American League

Division Series, limiting his effectiveness. The Yankees won that first game by a score of 10-7.

Next, in Game 2, the Red Sox elected to start future Hall of Fame pitcher Pedro Martinez. After the Yankees struck early with a run in the first, Martinez and Yankees pitcher Jon Lieber dueled for the victory on the mound. The Yankees added two runs in the sixth inning, and although the Red Sox finally got on the board with a run in the eighth inning, their offense dried up. The Yankees won Game 2 and led the series 2-0.

Game 3 was a rollercoaster. After the Yankees scored three in the first inning, the Red Sox responded with four of their own in the second. The Yankees retook the lead in the third, then Boston tied it in the bottom of the third. The fourth inning, though, was when the Yankees scored five and took a commanding lead. With 19 runs on 22 hits, the Yankees won Game 3 by a score of 19-8. They had a 3-0 lead, embarrassing the Red Sox in the process.

No team had ever come back from a 3-0 deficit.

Never.

At this point in baseball history, no team had even reached a Game 7 after falling behind 3-0.

Still, the Red Sox had to try. Game 4 in Boston followed the pattern of the rest of the series, in that the Yankees scored first. With two runs in the third inning, Red Sox fans were anxious, hoping they were not witnessing another heartbreaking end to their season.

Then, there was a sign of life from the Boston bats in the bottom of the fifth inning, sparked by a David Ortiz single to center field with the bases loaded, scoring two of the three runs in the inning to give the Red Sox the lead.

However, that lead was very short-lived, as the Yankees scored twice in the sixth to regain their advantage, 4-3. With zero runs scored in the seventh and eighth innings, the Red Sox were down to their final three outs.

Legendary closer Mariano Rivera was on the mound for the Yankees, looking to secure another trip to the World Series. If you're familiar with the Yankees' success in the 2000s, then you know about Mariano Rivera and his ability to close out games.

Then, something unexpected happened.

Kevin Millar was up first for the Red Sox, and he earned a walk, representing the tying run.

Dave Roberts came in as a pinch runner, and he stole second base on Rivera's first pitch to Bill Mueller. Mueller came through in the clutch, hitting a single that scored Roberts and tied the game. The Red Sox fans went wild, excited that not all hope was lost.

The game remained tied until the bottom of the 12th inning, when David Ortiz hit a two-run home run to win the game.

Game 5 began just 16 hours after Game 4 had concluded, and the Red Sox continued with their little bit of momentum, scoring two runs in the bottom of the first to take the early lead. The Yankees got one back in the second inning, then scored three in the sixth to take a 4-2 lead. The Red Sox responded in the bottom of the eighth with two runs to tie the game. And, just like Game 4, the teams needed extra innings to determine a winner.

This time, it took even longer. In the bottom of the 14th inning, Ortiz played the hero once again, singling to center field and bringing home Johnny Damon to score and win.

The Red Sox were halfway to a comeback victory, but there was a lot of work remaining.

In Game 6, Curt Schilling returned to the mound in what would become known as "The Bloody Sock Game."

Schilling was playing with a torn tendon sheath that was sutured to hold it in place. He pitched seven solid innings in the game, and when he left the mound after seven innings with only one run on the board for the Yankees, blood was visibly staining the white sock around his right ankle.

As for the Red Sox offense, they scored four runs in the top of the fourth inning, and that would be enough to maintain the lead and win by a score of 4-2.

The Boston Red Sox made baseball history by becoming the first team to force a Game 7 after trailing 3-0 in the series. But they were not done.

Game 7 was in Yankee Stadium, just as Game 6 had been. This time, though, the Sox were ready, jumping out to a 2-0 lead in the first inning thanks to another Ortiz home run. Then, Johnny Damon added to the lead in the top of the second inning with a grand slam. The Yankees got one run back in the third inning, but the Red Sox added on two more runs in the top of the fourth inning.

After two scoreless innings, the Yankees tried to close the gap with two runs in the seventh, but the Red Sox shut the door, adding a run in the eighth and ninth for insurance. By the end of the game, the Red Sox had a seven-run lead, and it was too much for the Yankees to overcome. Boston had taken their momentum and rode it all the way back from the brink.

The Red Sox became the first-ever MLB team to come back from such a deficit, earning a trip to the World Series. Riding the high of one of the most incredible feats ever accomplished, the Red Sox went on to sweep the St. Louis Cardinals in four straight games to win the World Series crown.

Did You Know?

1. David Ortiz was the first player with two walk-off home runs in one playoff run.

2. Yankees manager Joe Torre said he did not know how bad Schilling's injury was in Game 6, or he would have had his players bunt more often to make Schilling field the ball.

3. The 86 runs scored during the series are the most for any seven-game series in the history of baseball.

4. The Red Sox were the first MLB team to win eight playoff games in a row during the same playoff season.

5. At that time, the only other North American professional sports teams to overcome a 3-0 deficit were the 1942 Toronto Maple Leafs and the 1975 New York Islanders.

6. David Ortiz was named MVP of the series.

CHAPTER 21:

THE HAND OF GOD

Throughout the history of international soccer, teams and players representing their countries have accomplished great things, bringing happiness to the people back home. Perhaps most controversial was a particular goal scored by Diego Maradona. La mano de Dios, or "The Hand of God," was the name given to a controversial goal scored during the 1986 FIFA World Cup.

But the story doesn't start on the pitch that day. Many trace the rivalry back to the 1966 World Cup when England and Argentina played each other during the quarterfinals. In a match that featured a lot of fouls and excessive physicality, Argentina player Antonio Rattin was sent off for an egregious foul. Rattin was angry that the referee did not speak Spanish, assuming that the German referee was biased toward the European team, favoring England over the team from the other side of the world. As Rattin left the pitch, he stomped on the royal carpet in the stadium.

This act was seen as a sign of disrespect by the English. The team's manager, Alf Ramsey, described the Argentina players as "animals," which the Argentines considered to be a racist remark. From there, the two teams became bitter rivals, and matches between them were always full of emotion and anger. However, more events off the pitch would add to the fire later.

The 1986 match even involved events from four years earlier on the battlefield. The two teams involved in the World Cup match featuring the Hand of God goal are the same two countries that fought a two-month-long war over the Falkland Islands. England and Argentina battled over two territories in the South Atlantic Ocean that both countries claimed as their own. Argentina invaded the areas on April 2, 1982. Three days later, the British government sent a navy unit to engage with their opponents. For 74 days, the two countries fought over these areas.

Ultimately, the British defeated the Argentine forces and caused the downfall of the military government in Argentina, pushing the country toward the founding of a democracy.

Sentiments between the two countries were not friendly for quite a long time. This translated to the soccer pitch four years later.

Argentina defeated South Korea 3-1 to open their tournament, then played Italy to a 1-1 draw. To finish their group stage, Argentina defeated Bulgaria 2-0, securing the group stage victory. England began their tournament with a disappointing loss to Portugal, 1-0. They followed up their loss with a 0-0 tie against Morocco, but they thrashed Poland 3-0 to advance out of the group stage.

In the round of 16, Argentina managed a 1-0 win over Uruguay, while England was beginning to find their legs. A 3-0 victory over Paraguay set up the match between England and Argentina.

At this point in the tournament, the 24 teams that entered the contest were down to eight. In the quarter finals, England and Argentina were facing off in a rematch of the Falklands War, and Argentina was determined to score some retribution for the defeat their country was handed by the English.

The first half was tense and closely played, but neither team could find the opening strike. Argentina had controlled the possession for much longer, but they also did a lot more running. Some analysts wondered if England would have the advantage in the second half with their legs still fresh. After halftime, though, Argentina captain Diego Maradona was out to prove his country deserved better than England had treated them during the war.

Six minutes into the half, Jorge Valdano received a pass from Maradona but was swarmed by England defenders. After the ball bounced up, English midfielder Steve Hodge struck the ball back toward his goalkeeper, Peter Shilton. The ball was arcing high in the air, but Maradona ran up to contest its landing with the England keeper. Though Shilton was eight inches taller than Maradona, when the two players jumped up, it appeared as though Maradona had caught the ball with his head, knocking it past the keeper and into the goal.

Maradona began his celebration but also checked the reactions of the referee and linesman to see if the goal counted, and when it was confirmed, he went into full celebration mode. Several of the England defenders immediately swarmed the referee to argue that Maradona had struck the ball with his hand, which was tucked close to his head at the point of impact with the ball.

The referee consulted with his linesman but ultimately concluded that the goal would stand. England players were furious, but there was not much else to be done about the situation. As for Maradona and Argentina, they were determined to keep pushing the pace.

Four minutes later, seemingly empowered by his earlier goal, Diego Maradona scored a goal that many have named the Goal of the Century. Maradona collected the ball near the center of the field, then proceeded to dribble past five England players on his own before dribbling past the keeper and tucking the ball easily into the goal. In ten seconds, Maradona had run 60 yards, beaten half of the English team by himself, then scored a goal to beat them on the scoresheet. Argentina had a two-goal lead and only allowed a goal from England in the 81st minute. It would not be enough, though, and England was knocked out of the tournament.

After the match, when asked about the controversial goal, Diego Maradona half-joked that the ball was hit "a little with the head of Maradona and a little with the hand of God." This, of course, is where the goal gets its name. The Argentinians were not upset with Maradona's goal. In fact, they were happy that the controversy had caused so much pain for the English. Maradona himself considered the goal "some sort of symbolic revenge against the English."

Argentina, for their part, would go on to win the World Cup, with Maradona named as the best player of the tournament. They did not lose a match during that tournament, showing how dominant they had been for those few weeks of play.

After the tournament, though, controversy would cloud Argentina's victory, especially when a photo taken by Mexican photographer Alejandro Ojeda Carbajal showed in undeniable fashion that Maradona had indeed used his arm to strike the ball over the England keeper.

The soccer world was not so mad at Maradona for his handball goal to overlook his Goal of the Century four minutes later. The world still recognized that they had witnessed something brilliant happen on the pitch, even if that same player had cheated to score just moments earlier.

Since that 1986 quarterfinal, the two countries have met twice during World Cup play. During the 1998 World Cup, the teams faced off in the round of 16. Argentina got the best of England in a penalty shootout. Famously, David Beckham was sent off in that match.

In 2002, England would get some revenge of their own when Beckham's penalty kick goal was the only score during the two countries' group stage match. England would reach the quarterfinals of that tournament while Argentina was eliminated in the group stage.

Though the two teams have traded barbs and victories on the pitch over the last 60 years, no one can change the incredible and controversial performance by Diego Maradona on that day in 1986. Maradona would later admit that he used his hand to play the ball, but his hatred for England would keep him from apologizing for the dishonest play.

Whatever you think about the Falklands War or the relationship between these two countries, there is no denying that the events between them set a perfect stage for controversy at the World Cup. It made for an incredible story, one that is still being shared today.

Did You Know?

1. Maradona's jersey from that match was sold for $9.2 million at auction, a record for sports memorabilia.

2. Argentina had to switch jerseys after the group stage because the cotton jerseys they brought were too hot for the Mexico weather.

3. Before the match, fans from both teams fought in Mexico City, and stolen England flags were shown off during Argentine league matches later in the year.

4. Colombia was supposed to host the tournament, but Mexico stepped in when they could not manage it.

5. Even Maradona's teammates thought he would be called for a handball on the infamous play, so none of them immediately went to celebrate the goal with him.

6. Maradona called the England players "the noblest in the world" for not knocking him down during his Goal of the Century run.

CHAPTER 22:

28-3

Many stories in this book feature underdogs shocking the world or teams finding a way back from the brink of elimination, but there's only one story that is truly broken into two halves. After all, if a football team is down 28-3 in the Super Bowl, you'd usually be able to go to bed early and catch the remaining highlights the next day, because the contest is over.

Then, on one magical, incredible night, it wasn't over. This chapter centers on Super Bowl LI between the Atlanta Falcons and the New England Patriots on February 5, 2017. With 111 million viewers watching from around the world, something special was about to happen.

Let's see how it unfolded.

From the National Football Conference, the Atlanta Falcons, with an 11-5 record, emerged after victories against the Seattle Seahawks and Green Bay Packers. It was Atlanta's first playoff appearance in three years, marking a huge improvement with talented quarterback Matt Ryan under center. In fact, Ryan was named league MVP that year for his outstanding performance, and many considered the Falcons' offense to be too much for the Patriots to handle. The Falcons led the NFL in scoring with 540 points.

Second-year coach Dan Quinn had a lot to do with the team's newfound success, but some wondered if he had enough experience to bring the team all the way to the championship.

On the other side of the ball, the New England Patriots finished the regular season with the league's best record at 14-2, only losing to the Buffalo Bills and Seattle Seahawks. They had the league's best defense and the third-best offense. Impressively, they went 3-1 to start the season while future Hall of Fame quarterback Tom Brady served a four-game suspension for the controversy known as Deflategate, in which Brady was accused of letting air out of footballs to help his grip.

The Patriots also lost their All-Star tight end, Rob Gronkowski, in Week 13 due to a back injury. Somehow, the Patriots kept the wheels on the bus and cruised into the postseason, defeating the Houston Texans and Pittsburgh Steelers to reach the ultimate game.

To begin the game, both teams seemed tentative, not wanting to make an early big mistake and worsen their chances of a victory. Each team punted the ball twice in the first quarter, and the longest play of the opening frame belonged to Falcons running back Devonta Freeman, who had a 37-yard run.

In the second quarter, Brady and the Patriots got down to the 33-yard line of the Falcons after a 27-yard catch by Julian Edelman. However, on the very next play, LeGarrette Blount had the ball stripped away by Falcon's linebacker Deion Jones.

After two passes from Ryan to Julio Jones for a total of 42 yards, Freeman got the next three play calls and found the endzone on a five-yard run. The Falcons were up 7-0.

After a quick Patriots three-and-out, the Falcons offense continued flying. Ryan completed a 24-yard pass to Taylor Gabriel, then an 18-yard pass to Jones. On a long third down, Ryan found Austin Hooper in the endzone, doubling their lead to 14 points.

Tom Brady and company had never faced a 14-point deficit in the Super Bowl.

The Patriots' offense found some rhythm on the next possession, with some help from the referees. The Falcons' defense committed three holding penalties, and each of those penalties happened on third downs, giving Brady and the Patriots' offense a fresh set of downs to work with.

On third down, needing six yards from the Falcons' 23-yard line, a Brady pass was picked off by cornerback Robert Alford and returned 82 yards for another Atlanta touchdown. The lead was now 21 points, and things were not looking good for the Patriots.

With a little over two minutes left in the second quarter, New England was desperate to get some points on the board before halftime. A 15-yard pass to Martellus Bennett and a 28-yard pass to James White helped that effort, but the offense ran out of luck at the Falcons' 20-yard line. Stephen Gostkowski kicked a field goal to end the half, with the score 21-3 in favor of Atlanta.

It is often said that the better coach will make the adjustments necessary to win a football game at halftime. While the media does not often have access to the locker rooms during halftime, it's safe to say that some changes were made, though it took a while for the Patriots to find life. However, could a halftime adjustment make up for the 18-point deficit they were facing?

Both teams had chances early in the second half, but the best chance went to the Patriots after Edelman returned a punt nearly to midfield, giving Brady great field position. Unfortunately for the Patriots, they did not get a first down on that drive and had to give the ball back to Atlanta.

Starting from their own 15-yard line, the Falcons picked up right where they left off in the first half. Ryan connected with Gabriel twice, one for 17 and the second for 35 yards. Nearing the red zone, the Falcons only needed four more plays to reach the endzone again. This time, it was a six-yard pass to Tevin Coleman, another running back for the Falcons, making the score 28-3 with eight and a half minutes left in the third quarter.

Twenty-five points.

Remember, Brady had never faced a 14-point deficit in the Super Bowl. But 25 points? The task was gargantuan!

Beginning from their own 25-yard line, Brady and his offense went back to work. Short passes to Dion Lewis and James White got them a total of 14 yards, out to their own 39. Lewis then found a gap for an eight-yard run as the Patriots neared midfield. But, after another run was stuffed at the line, and an incomplete pass from Edelman, the Patriots faced fourth down, three yards to gain. Brady found Danny Amendola on a short pass left for a 17-yard gain.

From Atlanta's 37-yard line, Brady passed to Amendola for two more yards, then couldn't connect with Edelman on second down. On third down, Brady had to scramble away from tacklers, but he found a lot of open space ahead of him. He ran 15 yards to the 20-yard line of the Falcons. From there, LeGarrette Blount pounded the ball at the line, running for five, nine, and two yards to the Atlanta five. Brady then found White with the touchdown pass.

The score was 28-9 after a missed field goal by Gostkowski.

On the ensuing kickoff, with only a couple of minutes left in the third quarter, the Patriots attempted an onside kick to regain possession, but they failed and were penalized for an illegal touch. This mishap gave the Falcons the ball at the New England

41-yard line. A nine-yard pass moved the ball to the New England 32 before a sack and a penalty forced Atlanta to punt from their own 44.

The Patriots had the ball to start the fourth quarter, still down 19 points.

Malcolm Mitchell caught two passes for 22 yards total, then White ran for six yards. Brady looked for Edelman deep but couldn't connect, so he went back to Mitchell for another 18 yards. With 13 minutes left in the game, they were at the Atlanta 41. A short pass to White got them to the 32, then Brady connected with Bennett for 25 yards, down to the Atlanta 7.

After a couple of sacks, the Patriots settled for a field goal. The score was 28-12. The two teams were separated by 16 points with less than ten minutes left in the game.

The Patriots didn't try another onside kick, so the Falcons started at their own 27 after a decent kick return. Tevin Coleman gained eight yards on the ground, setting up second and short. He got one yard on the next run but was injured. On third and one yard to gain, Ryan went back to throw but was sacked and fumbled the ball. Dont'a Hightower forced the fumble with the sack, and the ball was recovered by Alan Branch.

The Patriots had the ball on the Falcons 25.

But on the first down, Brady was sacked for a loss of five yards. On second down, a pass to White was only good for four yards, setting up third-and-11. Yet Brady connected with Mitchell once more for 12 yards and a first down at the Atlanta 14. Brady passed to Amendola for eight yards, then caught another for the touchdown.

Using a direct snap to White on the two-point conversion, the Patriots were able to get a good push at the line for White to slip across and get the score.

The Falcons' lead was down to eight with over five minutes left in the game. That's only one more possession. Could the Patriots finish the comeback?

If they had a chance to pull it off, they first needed their defense to get a stop.

Gostkowski kicked off and forced the Atlanta return player to catch the ball at the three-yard line and attempt a return. After seven yards, the return man ran out of bounds, giving Matt Ryan the ball at his own ten-yard line with 5:53 left on the clock. All Atlanta had to do was get a few first downs and drain the clock.

Or they could get big plays and just win the game. On the first play from scrimmage, Ryan passed the ball short left to Freeman, who ran up the field for 39 yards to midfield. Freeman gained two yards on the next play, then Ryan connected with Julio Jones for a big 27-yard gain. Atlanta was at New England's 22-yard line a minute into their drive.

On first down, Freeman was stuffed at the line and lost a yard. Second down, Ryan gets sacked by Trey Flowers, backing up the Falcons to the New England 35-yard line, and suddenly, points don't feel like a guarantee on this drive.

Facing third and 23 yards to gain, Atlanta is penalized for holding, backing them up to the New England 45. Then, an incomplete pass forces Atlanta to punt the ball back to Brady and the Patriots with 3:38 left on the clock. After a fair catch by Edelman, the Patriots had the ball on their own nine-yard line.

They needed 91 yards and a two-point conversion to tie the game.

It was clear early that it was going to be a pass-heavy drive. Brady missed on first and second down to start the drive, then found Chris Hogan for 16 yards to move the chains. After another incompletion, he connected with Mitchell for 11 yards and another first down. Then Brady hit Edelman with a deep pass for 23 yards to Atlanta's 41.

Just before the two-minute warning, Brady struck with a pass to Amendola for 20 more yards. At the two-minute warning, the Patriots were already in the red zone, and there was a sense of inevitability beginning to set in for the Falcons.

Brady passed to White for 13 yards, then again for seven more before allowing White to punch it in from a yard out.

The score was 28-26 with 57 seconds left. A failed conversion would end the game.

Edelman, Hogan, and Amendola were out wide left. When the ball was snapped, Atlanta was flagged for offsides, but Brady still passed to Amendola, who barely broke the plane as Hogan and Edelman tried to block their defenders.

The game was tied. Atlanta tried to get the ball moving down the field for a winning field goal but couldn't get the passes to connect. The Super Bowl was going to overtime.

New England got the ball first in overtime, but you already know what happened next. Brady completed five straight passes for 50 yards, then a defensive pass interference call brought the ball to the Atlanta two-yard line, where White ultimately got the ball across the line to win the Super Bowl.

The greatest comeback in the history of professional football was complete. Tom Brady put the team on his shoulders and threw his way to another championship. New England's defense found their teeth in the second half and helped give the offense a chance.

It was an incredible game on all accounts, and it is considered to be one of the best Super Bowl games in football history.

Did You Know?

1. This Super Bowl was the sixth to feature the top offense against the top defense.

2. Former American President George H.W. Bush performed the coin toss.

3. Before this game, Tom Brady had played 33 playoff games without throwing an interception returned for a touchdown.

4. Brady's run of 15 yards was the longest-running play by the Patriots in the game.

5. This was the first Super Bowl game to go to overtime.

6. No team has ever come back from a 17-point deficit in the playoffs until the Patriots did it in this game.

CONCLUSION

There you have it. Twenty-two of the most incredible sports stories ever told, each one special and incredible for its own reasons. Perhaps you enjoyed a good comeback story, like the outrageous comeback by the New England Patriots, or the Shot Heard 'Round the World by the New York Giants.

Perhaps your favorite was the Red Sox and their miraculous comeback against their archrivals, the New York Yankees. Comeback stories are great because they show us that even when we are at our lowest, if our hearts are still beating, we can fight back. We can dig ourselves out of these holes we're in. These incredible comebacks remind us of one thing: there's still a chance.

If comebacks aren't your thing, maybe you connect with the athletes who shifted the social or political landscape with their achievements and talents.

For example, consider the great female athletes who changed their sports for the better, like Rousey, Sorenstam, and Williams. They showed the world that their skill and talent is worth watching. Jackie Robinson also affected American culture by breaking the color barrier in baseball, the biggest sport in the country.

All these special athletes teach us that we don't have to accept the world exactly as it is. We can fight to make it better by setting an example and following through.

Whichever story you found to be the most entertaining, there is one truth that permeates through all of this: humans are capable of greatness. When you see your favorite athlete pull off the impossible, it makes you realize that you, too, are capable of great things.

This book sought to capture some of the biggest moments in professional sports history, from a wide range of sports. However, this is by no means a complete list.

There are plenty of winners and champions not featured in these pages, but you can always look for more stories to add to your personal collection. After all, an inspiring sports story can help you achieve greatness for yourself.

The world of sports is full of amazing stories that need to be remembered. Go find the one that will inspire you to push forward.

Made in the USA
Las Vegas, NV
11 December 2024

13891127R00098